MAKING
MOBILES

First published in the United
Kingdom in 2020 by
Pavilion
An imprint of
HarperCollins*Publishers*
1 London Bridge Street
London SE1 9GF

www.harpercollins.co.uk

HarperCollins*Publishers*
Macken House
39/40 Mayor Street Upper
Dublin 1
D01 C9W8
Ireland

ISBN 978-1-91164-163-6

A CIP catalogue record for
this book is available from the
British Library.

10 9 8 7 6 5 4 3

Reproduction by Rival Colour
Ltd, UK
Printed and bound by
Papercraft, Malaysia

www.pavilionbooks.com

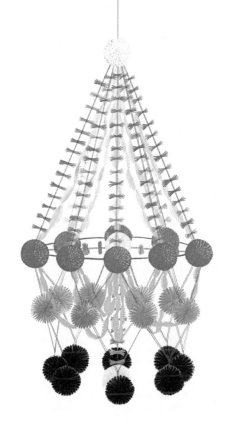

MAKING
MOBILES

Create beautiful Polish pajaki from natural materials

KAROLINA MERSKA

PAVILION

MY SEARCH FOR MOBILES

Steeped in history and symbolism, Polish mobiles are enchanting folk decorations, traditionally made from straw, paper, wool, feathers and dried peas. Variations can be found all over Eastern Europe, and even in Scandinavia, but none are as bright or colourful as the Polish ones.

Back home, these mobiles are called *pająk* (pronounced 'pah-yonk') or *pająki* (the plural).

Delicate and light, these chandeliers would often hang from ceilings around wintertime, spinning gently when a stray draft would breeze through the home. Unfortunately, their origin and full history is difficult to uncover, as not many original early designs survive today. Their scarcity drives my passion to keep the pająki tradition alive.

My own story with mobiles starts in the Open Air Village Museum in Lublin, Poland, where I first saw pająki hanging in one of the traditional village houses. Then, years later, while studying History of Art at the Jagiellonian

University in Kraków, in addition to my studies on medieval and modern art I developed an interest in the ethnography and history of traditional Polish folk culture. It has now become a sort of obsession – I even called my own art and interiors shop, in London, Folka – which is a portmanteau of *Polka* (Polish girl) and 'folk'.

I kept thinking about pająki – a perfect mix of bold colours that demanded attention, but were fragile to the touch – I just couldn't get them out of my mind. But it wasn't until the summer of 2015 in London (where I had moved to in 2007) that I finally made my first pająk. I have to say that it wasn't the best thing ever, but practice always makes perfect.

First I experimented with a straw structure. When I had finished, everything looked great, but as soon as I lifted the mobile to hang it, all the layers folded inside so I had to start again from the beginning. This was when I realized how important it is to begin with a solid structure.

Since then, I have improved my skills and have started to teach my own classes on how to make pająki.

I love revisiting traditional techniques and materials, as well as experimenting with new ones, to give my mobiles a contemporary look. In addition to using rye straw, which I harvest myself each summer in Poland (I make sure I store it away properly – mice love the taste of it!), I also use brass tubes, to give that chic interiors look. I don't always want to copy old designs – our modern interpretations of folk art can always generate exciting pieces!

Nowadays, pająki making is a dying craft in Poland, practised primarily by elderly women, who were taught by their mothers and grandmothers. You can see their work mainly in ethnography museums or during folk craft festivals. In Poland, young people don't really know the story of the tradition and even find them tacky and old fashioned. Beauty like this shouldn't gather dust in a museum, so I wanted to revitalize them and show that you could hang them in a modern home.

I love teaching people about pająki and running workshops in my studio and beyond. It's very rewarding to see so many new faces come to my classes, eager to learn, and me, eager to teach. Nothing beats a fun afternoon fashioning pompoms out of tissue paper, with good coffee and good conversation. But, not only is it a fun group activity to do, it brings me so much joy to see that the pająki tradition is being revived. There's something magical in that.

A very important part of my practice is to travel to Poland to meet artists who still make pająki. Meeting them is always inspiring and I learn a lot about the history through their memories. It's important to say that mobile making has been passed down through generations. Families used to make pająki together, but sadly, this is not so common anymore.

I am so excited that I can share this book with you. I will

teach you different types of pająki – traditional, as well as contemporary ones – to show you the wealth of different designs you can create!

I highly recommend that you have a full read through of any project that takes your fancy and practise making the individual components. Making mobiles takes quite a bit of time, so it is a good idea to become familiar with making the arms and pompoms and have them ready before you start building the structure.

Another very important part of the book for me is to present to you three lovely artists and their stories: Helena (p82), Zofia (p100) and Józef (p166). Their beautiful designs deserve a place in this book, as I owe them so much for their guidance and advice.

PAJĄKI & POLAND

A long time ago, the pająk was a common feature inside the traditional wooden cottages in Poland. A breathtaking showstopper, the mobile would have been suspended from a beam in the central living space, spinning delicately, complementing the other colourful folk ornaments in the house; paper cut-outs, also known as *wycinanki*; paintings adorned with paper flowers and enchanting, hand-painted wallhangings. The pająk was not only a beautiful object, it also had symbolic significance.

Constructed of rye straw and paper, mobiles became a popular decoration at the turn of the 19th century. Made largely by women, they were the perfect ornaments to brighten up the home and could be made relatively easily, with a little bit of elbow grease. The Polish name, *pająk*, literally translates as 'spider'. Although the etymology of the name is not clear. Old legends say that finding a spider in the home was a sign of good luck – these days, it's still considered bad luck to kill a spider. During my research into the history of pająki, I had met with Professor Marian Pokropek, who brought to my attention that 'pająk' was also an old name for the decorative chandeliers that hang in churches and palaces (according to a 1901 edition of *Encyklopedia Staropolska* by Zygmunt Gloger). I think I prefer the spider theory myself – it's more evocative and it helps to explain the symmetrical, web-like quality to their shape.

Straw at Christmas

Straw is the key element of a pająk and rye is the best to use because of its length and strength. Not only that, rye was an important part of country life, as every harvest, the straw would be cut down, traditionally with a scythe. Straw was everything to the people working on the land – so much so that, at the time, they believed that it had magical powers. It's no surprise, as they were wholly dependant on their fields and crops, which provided them with food and pasture for

their livestock. They would make beautiful straw wreaths as well as larger decorative structures to celebrate the end of harvesting and give thanks for the yield.

After the harvest, the very last stalks of grain would be neatly tied together and the sheaf (called *dziad*) was stored until December. Extra pieces of straw were kept to be used later on for making pająki and other decorations – mobiles were always made for Christmas.

During Christmas straw would also be scattered on the floor and under the table to protect the house from evil spirits and demons. Essentially, the belief was that a straw pająk hanging above the table was supposed to bring a good harvest, prosperity and happiness in the coming year.

After Christmas, new pająki were made for Easter celebrations. The Christmas pająk was burned as a symbol of a new chapter and to affirm the reawakening of nature. Very often, Easter pająki were adorned with *pisanki* (decorated Easter eggs) instead of flowers or pompoms. Pająki were also made for other celebrations, such as weddings and christenings.

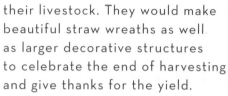

Shapes & structures

The shapes and structures of pajāki were largely determined by what materials were available at the time. The earliest known pajāki designs (called *sowa* or 'owl') were spherical; long pieces of rye straw with hand-cut paper circles or stars attached on top were pressed into a potato, beetroot or a round piece of wax or dough – common items that could be found around the home.

In time, the pajāk's structure became more decorative. Inspired by large metal chandeliers in churches, women devised new ideas of how to build larger designs. The arms of the mobiles were threaded with short pieces of straw, pine cone scales, beans and even different varieties of feathers in Masovia (east-central Poland). and then attached to the main circular structure, made of willow or twisted wire. In Podlasie (north-eastern Poland), interesting pajāki were made using only strips of white fabric.

Another popular shape of pajāk is a geometric one, created from one large central pyramid, traditionally adorned with five smaller ones. Geometric designs are also known in other countries: Estonia, Belarus, Lithuania (*sodas*), Ukraine (*pavuk*) and Finland (*himmeli*). Only in Poland were structures decorated with paper flowers. If you fancy making a geometric masterpiece for yourself, check out the projects on p84 and p182.

At the turn of the 20th century, new materials became available, like coloured papers and ribbons, so the pajāki designs became more and more colourful and elaborately decorated with different types of paper pompoms and flowers. I know whenever I go into a craft shop, I can't help buying all the beautiful papers I find!

Łowicz (in central Poland) is famous for its rich folklore, unique paper cut-outs and handwoven embroidered costumes. Elements of these garments have been incorporated into pajāki designs: instead of a round structure, these have a polygonal, handwoven wool platform with the famous Łowicz bright and colourful stripes. I've shown you how to make a traditional Łowicz pajāk on p108.

Unique designs were also made in Kurpie (north-eastern Poland). This region has its own traditional folk heritage and dialect. Hence the pająk here is called *kierec* and is made with threaded peas or beans attached to round wire structures adorned with beautiful paper flowers. If you have any pulses or even beads around the house, you can make one yourself following the steps on p102. The word 'pająk' in Kurpie instead meant a structure attached to the ceiling – long strips of twisted paper were gathered in the centre of the of the room, spread out and pinned around the outside.

In Zalipie (south-eastern Poland) – known as the 'painted village' because of its traditional cottages hand-painted with colourful floral motifs – pająki were decorated with varieties of colourful flowers.

MAKING A PAJĄK

The most traditional pająki were made from rye straw and paper. In this book I will show you different varieties of shapes and ways to decorate your pająk. Once you know how to create the structure you can start experimenting with other materials to design your own unique pająk. I should to mention that you should take your time making a pająki. A simple design like the Kalinka Pająk (p68) takes me about half a day to finish, while a larger-scale project like the Master Pająk (p120), may take over a week to finish. Wishing you good luck and lots of patience in your pająki-making adventure!

MATERIALS & TOOLS

These are the materials and tools that I have used to make my
pająki. Some things are essential (pp22-25), but please feel free
to experiment with other trimmings.

1 Tissue paper
(p23)
2 Card (p23)
3 Crepe paper
(p23)
4 Glue
5 Metal hoops
(p25)
6 Compass

7 Pencil
8 White dried
peas (p22)
9 Foil
10 Cotton
crochet thread
(p25)
11 Ruler
12 Scissors

13 Sharpener
14 6cm (2½ in.)
sewing needles
15 Pins
16 Rye straw
(p22)
17 Thread snips
18 Spoon
19 Paper punch

Also useful for some projects:
tube cutter, ribbon, ric rac trim,
wool yarn, wooden dowel rods,
florist wire, jute macramé twine,
drinking straws, pasta, fabric
glue, 5mm (¼ in.) brass tubes,
felt beads, glass beads, metal
wire, cutting pliers.

Rye straw

This is the most important material in your pająk. I use rye straw as it's the strongest and the longest type. It should ideally be cut during harvest season using a scythe. But naturally not everyone has access to a wheat field and a scythe, so you can use paper drinking straws instead, as I have done on p144.

Before using straw for a pająk you need to prepare it: cut off the rye ears and clean each piece by removing the thin outer layers. Then, cut each long piece into shorter ones, as it's easier to store. Later on, you can cut them to the length you need.

Use only strong pieces of straw; do not use pieces that are too soft, as they will break easily.

Tip If ever a piece of straw breaks in your pająk, don't worry. You can cut a tiny piece of clear tape and wrap it around the broken piece so it holds it together.

Dried peas

I've used these for Zofia's Kierec on p102. It is important is to buy dried white peas with the skin on. You can find these in larger supermarkets, health stores or online.

They need to soak overnight to become soft before you can use them. Fill up half a bowl (approximately 15cm/6 in. diameter) with dried peas and then cover them with water. In the morning you can start threading them for your pająk.

You can also use dried beans (white or brown). Soak them in the same way.

Paper

In addition to the rye straw, paper is another very important material for pająki making. You can never have too much! I love choosing and collecting new colours so I always visit any stationery or craft stores that I come across, to check if they have any different papers.

For pająki making, you will need at least three different types of paper:

Tissue paper

This is the thin, smooth paper used for the pompoms (p34). It is very fragile and will tear easily. It comes in different quantities and sizes. When cutting tissue paper I recommend folding it beforehand, so that you can cut lots of layers at once. This works especially well for the pompoms – for example, if I have five large sheets, I fold it twice so I can cut 15 layers at once.

Crepe paper

This is wrinkly paper, which is thicker than tissue paper. It's sturdy and also stretchy, so it's perfect for making flowers (pp54-59) as well as for wrapping the hoop for your pająk (pp28-29). It usually comes in long rolls. You can cut the exact length you need by cutting a slice of the roll or if it's too difficult you can unroll it and then cut a piece to the size you need.

Card

This is used for making circles (p33). You need a thick card, 270gsm works best, but you can also use 175gsm. It comes in many different sizes, from small A4 sheets to A1. I usually buy larger sheets so it lasts longer and I can use it for different designs.

Scissors

You will need a pair of scissors, but I don't have any particular favourite type. I use a pair of sharp, vintage ones. It's important to get sharp scissors for paper with a comfortable handle. Sometimes when you are working on a larger pająk you will need to cut lots of layers for pompoms, and your hand can get quite tired! I recommend you go to a stationery shop, try different ones and choose the most comfortable pair you can find.

I also like using thread snips sometimes, especially when threading the pająki structure or adding pompoms.

Metal hoops

These are available from craft stores and come in a variety of different sizes. If you're planning to make a very large pająk you will need to commission a metalworker to have it specially made. Traditionally the hoops for pająki were made from wrapped wire or willow.

Thread

Use a soft, cotton crochet thread in a natural colour. Don't use a fine, synthetic thread as it can cut the straw pieces. I tend to measure lengths by eye. If in doubt, it is always better to have a piece that is too long than too short.

Paper punch

You can get these in so many shapes – squares, circle, stars, flowers, butterflies – so it depends on your imagination which one you want to use for your pająki's arms (p32). I like a traditional circle shape and I mostly use a 3cm (1¼ in.) or 4cm (1½ in.) one. Punches with larger diameters are perfect for using on bigger pająki. You can also combine two or more different sizes within your design – this will give your pająk a nice extra movement. While cutting out circles, try to cut them very close to one another so you don't waste paper.

STRUCTURE OF THE PAJĄK

It is important to understand the basic
structure of the pająk. A pająk is always made
up of the same basic elements, so bear this in
mind when designing your own. Before I start
to build a pająk, I always start by sketching it
out like this, it helps me to visualize it and to
finesse the design.

Upper arms

**Middle
platform**

Lower arms

While planning your pająk, the most important thing is to design its 'core' – the middle structure or the platform – which can be a metal hoop with crossed arms threaded with straw and circles or a woollen woven platform. Then I divide the pająk into upper and lower structures, and always start with the upper one.

Upper structure

This consists of a minimum of four outer arms, these are necessary for your pająk to hang. Then, depending on how decorative you want your pająk to be, you can add additional inside dangling arms and the middle arm (which goes through the whole pająk).

Tip Once I have finished making the pająk's upper arms, I usually hang it up, as this makes it easier to work on the lower structure.

Lower structure

This consists of different types of hanging arms, usually longer ones with pompoms or shorter dangling ones hanging between them.

Once your pająk's structure is ready, the last thing to do is to decorate your pająk with pompoms or paper flowers by attaching them to the middle platform.

Colours

At this stage I also plan out the colour scheme for my pająk. I tend to use fewer colours than is common in more traditional designs, which are often very colourful. I prefer to use lighter colours on the upper part and darker ones on the lower parts, I feel that this gives the design a nice depth. It is up to you how many colours you use, though, and you can always add more by making coloured arms, pompoms or flowers!

This book starts with a basic structure (p68) and then progresses to more challenging projects. This way, you'll learn how you can make your pająk bigger and more decorative by adding a larger hoop and more arms.

Wrapping a BASIC HOOP

The hoop is a very important part of your pająk as it holds the entire structure together. I usually wrap it with crepe paper as this covers the metal surface nicely.

What you will need

Crepe paper
Scissors
Metal hoop
Glue

1 Cut a 2cm (¾ in.) strip from a roll of crepe paper.

2 Apply a tiny amount of glue to the hoop and attach one end of the crepe paper strip. Hold the end down tightly and wrap the strip around the hoop. Crepe paper is flexible so you can pull it slightly at an angle to cover the hoop nicely. Overlap it as you go, so that the hoop underneath does not show.

3 Once you have wrapped the whole hoop, apply glue to the end of the crepe paper strip to secure it. Trim off any excess paper.

Note If you are wrapping a larger hoop, you may need to use more than one strip of paper.

Wrapping a FRINGED HOOP

Another option is to cover the hoop with a fringed paper. This is a traditional way of cutting paper – I like it a lot as it gives a nice extra volume to your pająk.

What you will need

Crepe paper
Scissors
Metal hoop
Glue

1 Cut a 3cm (1¼ in.) strip from a roll of crepe paper.

2 Keeping the strip folded, make a series of 1cm (½ in.) cuts, very close together, down one side.

3 Apply a tiny amount of glue to the hoop and attach one end of the crepe paper strip with the fringe side facing to the right.

4 Hold the end down tightly and wrap the strip around the entire hoop, as on p28.

ARM
TYPES

There are different ways
to decorate a pająk's arms.
In the past, the most popular
way to build arms was by
adding fluffy tissue paper
circles between pieces
of straw. I also like using
simple card circles as I think
they give the pająk a neat,
contemporary look. I have
included some beautiful,
now forgotten designs, like
Łowicz circles or fringed
crepe paper arms. While
planning your pająk decide
on your favourite designs
and then thread them on
with a needle, adding rye
or paper straw pieces in
between each time.

1 Fluffy circles

Using a compass and scissors or a 3cm (1¼ in.) circle punch, cut through ten layers of tissue paper to make each circle set. Make eight cuts around the edge using scissors, and pierce through the centre of the set with a needle. Fluff out the layers after threading.

2 Simple circles

Use a 3cm (1¼ in.) circle punch to cut the required number of shapes out of coloured card. You could also use different shapes: triangles, stars or flowers.

3 Łowicz circles

Using a compass and scissors or 3cm (1¼ in.) circle punch, cut out 20 layers of tissue paper to make each circle set. Follow steps 3–6 of the Tube Pompom method on pp48–49.

4 Threaded peas

Make sure you have soaked your peas overnight (p22). Thread a needle and pierce through the peas. Thread them close together and don't leave any space between them. After threading, allow the arms to hang for a day to dry out.

5 Foil balls

Cut 3cm (1¼ in.) foil squares and roll them into balls.

6 Paper fans

Cut a 10cm (4 in.) strip of crepe paper. The width of the strip will depend on how large you want your fans. Fold the paper in accordion style (fold, flip over, fold, flip over). Each fold can be around 7mm (¼ in.). When threading the fans, wrap the thread twice round the middle to give it a nicer shape.

7 Fringe

Cut a 3cm (1¼ in.) wide strip from a folded sheet of crepe paper. Make 2cm (¾ in.) cuts along one edge, close together. Then unfold the strip and cut it in whatever lengths you need.

THE POMPOMS

Traditional pająki wouldn't be so spectacular without paper pompoms. These are what makes a pająk's structure look so incredible and unforgettable. Pompoms come in different shapes and sizes and the colour options are endless – you can choose whatever you want!

In this section you will find a variety of traditional pompoms – the fluffy and flowery Kalinka Pompom, the spiky Hedgehog Pompom, and, my favourite (and perhaps the most challenging!), the Tube Pompom. I hope you will have fun making them.

Apart from being an important part of a pająk, you can also make these pompoms to use as single decorations – in the past they were sometimes hung on Christmas trees. They also look beautiful just hanging by a window.

KALINKA POMPOM

This beginner pompom is named *kalinka* after the globular flowers of the guelder rose shrub that can be found all over Eastern Europe.

Layers 15 · **Size** 10cm (4 in.) diameter

What you will need

Tissue paper
Ruler
Compass
Pencil
Needle
Scissors
Cotton crochet thread
Foil

Note If you are making pompoms to decorate a pająk, you will need to leave long threads for tying in place. To hang a single pompom, tie on a piece of ribbon and cut off the threads. For more information on how to tie on the ribbon, see step 5 on p45.

1 Take five sheets of tissue paper and fold them into thirds, one third on top of the other. This will create a pad of tissue that is 15 sheets thick. With a compass, draw a 10cm (4 in.) diameter circle on the tissue paper.

2 Pierce a needle through the centre of the circle to hold the layers together and cut it out.

3 With the layers still together (don't remove the needle), make eight equally spaced cuts around the edge of the circle, by cutting first at the quarter points and then dividing those in half. Cuts should finish 1cm (½ in.) from the needle.

4 Remove the needle and separate the layers. Then, taking the first layer, gently twist each segment through 180 degrees to make eight 'petals'.

5 Shape the end of each petal into a curve using your thumb and finger. Repeat these steps on the remaining layers. Cut a 50cm (19½ in.) length of thread, thread it onto a needle, fold it in half and tie the end with a knot. Wrap a tiny piece of foil around the knot.

6 Pull the needle through the centre of each piece. Alternate the layers so that one faces up and the next faces down, and so on. Make sure the petals are staggered, so you don't get any gaps. Once all the layers are threaded onto the needle, pull them down to the knot.

7 When you have threaded all the pieces, cut out a small, square piece of tissue paper (1cm/½ in.) and thread it onto the needle. Push the square down into the pompom to hold the layers in place. This acts as a stopper and will protect the tissue. Cut the needle off the thread and tie a double knot. Fluff out the layers with your fingers to make your pompom nice and round.

HEDGEHOG POMPOM

This is called the *jeżyk* (hedgehog) pompom because of its spikes!

Layers 12 · **Size** 10cm (4 in.) diameter

What you will need

Tissue paper

Ruler

Compass

Pencil

Pencil sharpener

Needle

Scissors

Glue

Cotton crochet thread

Foil

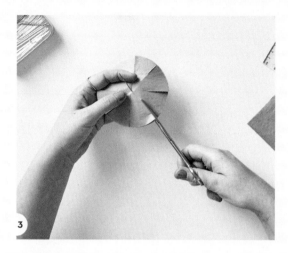

1 Take four sheets of tissue paper and fold them into thirds, one third on top of the other. This will create a pad of tissue that is 12 sheets thick. With a compass, draw a 10cm (4 in.) diameter circle on the tissue paper.

2 Pierce a needle through the centre of the circle to hold the layers together and cut it out.

3 With the layers still together (don't remove the needle), make eight equally spaced cuts around the edge of the circle, by cutting first at the quarter points and then dividing those in half. Cuts should finish 1cm (½ in.) from the needle.

4 Remove the needle and separate the layers. Taking the first layer, place a sharpened pencil in the middle of one of the eight segments. Line up the sharp tip of the pencil with the edge of the paper circle.

5 With one hand underneath, wrap the left corner of the tissue paper segment around the tip of the pencil.

6 Wrap the right corner of the tissue paper segment over the top, and secure in place with a tiny bit of glue. This will create a spiky petal.

7 Remove the pencil and continue to roll the remaining segments in the same way. Repeat these steps on the remaining tissue layers.

8 Cut a 50cm (19½ in.) length of thread, thread it onto a needle, fold it in half and tie the end with a knot. Wrap a tiny piece of foil around the knot.

9 Pull the needle through the centre of each piece, alternating the layers so that one faces up and the next faces down. Once all the layers are threaded onto the needle, pull them down to the knot.

10 When you have threaded all the pieces, cut out a small, square pad of tissue paper (1cm/½ in.) from 8–10 sheets of tissue paper and thread this onto the needle. Push it down into the pompom to hold the layers in place. This acts as a stopper and will protect the tissue. Cut the needle off the thread and tie a double knot to secure.

Józef's HEDGEHOG POMPOM

This is a special variation of the hedgehog pompom, made by a lovely folk artist named Józef. It is so special – he covers spikes of the pompom with foil so it looks like a snowflake. It makes a beautiful Christmas tree decoration or can be hung on its own.

Layers 12 • **Size** 10cm (4 in.) diameter

What you will need

White paper, for example
  A4 printer paper sheets
  (21 x 30cm/8¼ x 11¾ in.)
Ruler
Compass
Pencil
Pencil sharpener
Needle
Scissors
Foil
Glue
Cotton crochet thread
5mm (¼ in.) ribbon
  (optional)

1 Using sheets of white printer paper, and cutting out the circles of paper a few at a time, rather than working on 12 layers at once, follow steps 1–3 of the Hedgehog Pompom instructions on pp42–43.

2 Prepare 96 pieces of foil (one for each spiky petal), by cutting out small squares. They do not need to be exact, but they should all be around 2–3cm (¾–1¼ in.).

3 Create the spiky petals by following steps 4–7 on pp42–43. Wrap a piece of foil around the pointy end of each of the petals, securing it in place with a tiny bit of glue.

4 Thread the layers, following steps 8–9 on p43, using just two 1cm (½ in.) squares of paper as a stopper (this weight of paper is much stronger).

5 To make a single hanging pompom, take a 20cm (8 in.) length of ribbon, fold it in half and knot the ends together to make a loop. Fix it in place by pulling one of the threads through the centre of the loop, then tie with a strong double knot. Trim off the threads. Otherwise, leave the threads untrimmed to use on a pająk.

TUBE POMPOM

Although this may look daunting, and is certainly quite time-consuming, this is my favourite traditional paper pompom and definitely worth putting in the effort!

Layers 30 • **Size** 8cm (3¼ in.) diameter

What you will need

Tissue paper
Ruler
Compass
Pencil
Needle
Scissors
Spoon with a very flat,
  simple handle
Cotton crochet thread
Foil

1 Take five sheets of tissue paper and fold them into thirds, one third on top of the other. This will create a pad of tissues that is 15 sheets thick. Repeat with another five sheets, so you have two sets of 15 layers, ready to cut out.

2 With a compass, draw an 8cm (3¼ in.) diameter circle on the first set of tissue paper layers. Pierce a needle through the centre of the circle to hold the layers together and cut it out.

3 With the layers and needle still together, make 16 equally spaced cuts around the edge of the circle, by cutting first at the quarter points, then dividing those in half, and in half again. Cuts should finish 1cm (½ in.) from the needle.

4 Remove the needle, separate the layers and hold the first layer in your palm. Curl each segment using the flat handle of the spoon. Hold the handle parallel to the cut edge and roll it along the tissue, with an action almost like 'spreading butter'. This requires practice and patience. Roll each segment in the same way.

5 Repeat these steps on the remaining layers, and then on the second set of tissue, until you have worked through all 30 layers. Cut a 50cm (19½ in.) length of thread, thread it onto a needle, fold it in half and tie the end with a knot. Wrap a tiny piece of foil around the knot.

6 Pull the needle through the centre of each piece. Alternate the layers so that one faces up and the next faces down. Once all the layers are threaded onto the needle, pull them down to the knot.

6

7

7 When you have threaded all the pieces, cut out a small, square pad of tissue paper (1cm/½ in.) from 8–10 layers of tissue paper and thread this onto the needle. Push the squares down into the pompom to hold the layers in place. This acts as a stopper and will protect the tissue. Cut the needle off the thread and tie a double knot to secure.

TUBE Łowicz POMPOM

This is a beautiful variation of the tube pompom.
I call it 'Łowicz-style' as I discovered this type of
pompom at the unique Julian Brzozowski's Museum in
Sromów near Łowicz, in Poland. His wife Wanda made
pająki to decorate the space – the number and variety
was incredible. It was such an inspirational visit!

Layers 30 · **Size** 8cm (3¼ in.) diameter

What you will need

Tissue paper
Ruler
Compass
Pencil
Needle
Scissors
Spoon with a very flat,
  simple handle
Cotton crochet thread
Foil

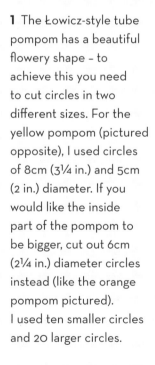

1 The Łowicz-style tube pompom has a beautiful flowery shape – to achieve this you need to cut circles in two different sizes. For the yellow pompom (pictured opposite), I used circles of 8cm (3¼ in.) and 5cm (2 in.) diameter. If you would like the inside part of the pompom to be bigger, cut out 6cm (2¼ in.) diameter circles instead (like the orange pompom pictured). I used ten smaller circles and 20 larger circles.

2 Follow steps 1–6 on pp48–49, using both the large and small circles (described in step 1, left).

3 Pull the needle through the centre of each piece, threading the smaller layers first followed by the larger ones. Alternate the layers so that one faces up and the next faces down.

4 Once you have threaded all the pieces, follow step 7 on p49 to finish.

KURPIE ROSE

This is a traditional paper rose made in the Kurpie region of Poland. Each flower is made of one piece of crepe paper twisted along one edge and then rolled into a flower shape.

Size 7cm (2¾ in.) diameter

What you will need

Crepe paper – one colour
   for the flower, green for
   the stem
Ruler
Scissors
Cotton crochet thread
15cm (6 in.) length of
   florist wire
Glue

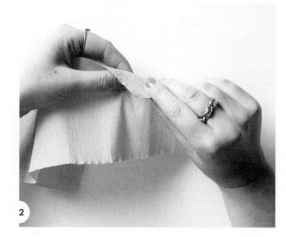

1 Cut a piece of crepe paper, 90 x 10cm (35½ x 4 in.). Lay the strip out in front of you, and fold the right corner over to make a triangle (around 4cm/1½ in.).

2 Holding the triangle down with your right thumb, fold another layer of paper down on top of the triangle, as shown.

3 Then, holding the new triangle tight at the bottom with your left thumb, twist your right hand away from you and unfold the paper, pressing it flat with your right thumb. Take care not to rip the paper. You need to achieve a round 'wave' shape.

4 Move your right thumb and hold the paper next to the 'wave'. Repeat steps 3a to 3c to create another 'wave'.

5 Continue along the whole length of paper.

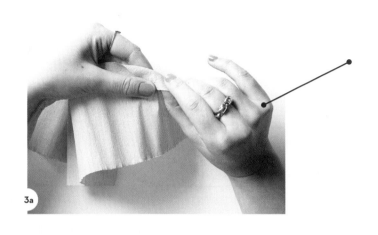

**Twist
your right
hand away
from you**

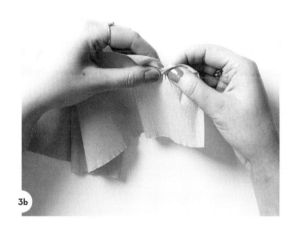

3b

3c

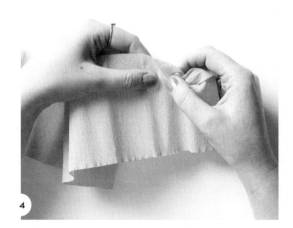

4

5

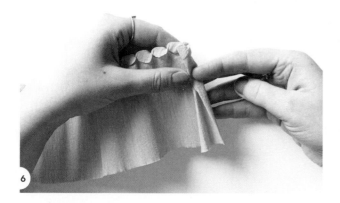

6 Once you have folded along the whole length of the strip, you need to start rolling it into a rose shape. Starting from the right end, fold the end of the strip in and slowly roll it towards the left.

7 Gently press the folded wavy edges on the 'outside' so the waves open up like a rose The flower should be flat on top, so while rolling make sure you adjust the layers with your fingers.

8 When you have finished rolling up the flower, cut a 10cm (4 in.) piece of thread, wrap it around the bottom of the flower and tie a strong double knot. Cut off the excess paper.

9 Take the piece of florist wire and wrap one end tightly around the thread a few times and bend the rest of the wire down to form a long stem. Cut a 4cm (1½ in.) strip of green crepe paper, and, with scissors, make a series of cuts halfway across the width of the paper. The cuts should be close together to create a fringe effect.

10 Apply a little glue to the bottom of the flower and around the wire and start wrapping the green fringed paper around the stem, starting at the flower.

11 Continue wrapping the wire stem until it is completely covered. Cut off any excess paper and glue the end of paper to the wire. Your rose is ready. It can be used for a bouquet or to decorate your pająk.

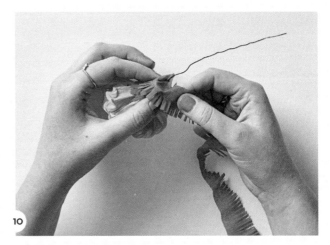

CARNATION FLOWER

I call this a carnation as its shape and fluffy appearance reminds me of those pretty flowers. These are perfect to decorate simple shapes, such as the Geometric Pająk (p84).

Layers 30 · **Size** 4cm (1½ in.)

What you will need

Tissue paper	Pencil	Cotton crochet
Ruler	Needle	thread
Compass	Scissors	Foil

1 Take ten sheets of tissue paper and fold them into thirds, one third on top of the other. This will create a pad of tissue that is 30 sheets thick. With a compass, draw a 4cm (1½ in.) diameter circle. Pierce a needle through the centre of the circle to hold the layers together and cut it out.

2 With the layers and needle still together, make four equally spaced cuts around the edge of the circle, at the quarter points. Cuts should finish 1cm (½ in.) from the needle.

3 Remove the needle, but keep the layers together. Fold the circle in half, at the point where two of the cuts are.

4 Make eight further cuts, four on each quarter. They will be quite close together.

5 Cut a 50cm (19½ in.) length of thread the needle, fold in half and make a knot at the bottom. Cut a tiny square of foil and wrap around the knot. Pull the needle through the centre of the layers. Cut out a small, square (1cm/½ in.) of tissue paper and thread onto the needle. Push the square down into the flower to hold the layers in place. Cut the thread, and tie a double knot.

6 Carefully fluff out the layers of the flower with your fingers until you are happy with the shape.

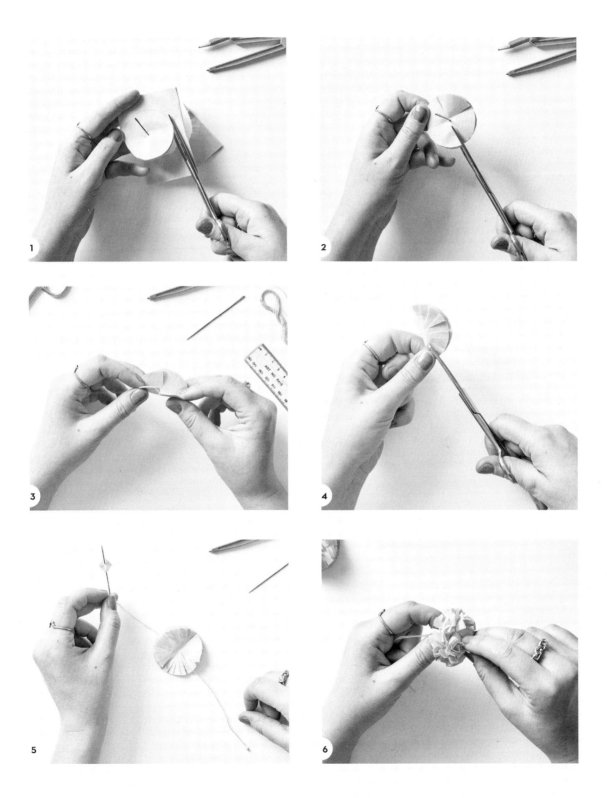

WOOLLEN POMPOMS & TASSELS

Woollen pompoms and tassels are a perfect way to add a modern twist to traditional pająki. It's such fun to create them using different coloured yarns. They're easy to make and add a beautiful texture to your design. They are ideal not only for a project for a child's nursery but also as part of a bigger installation for your living room.

What you will need

Pompom template (p190)
Thick paper or card
Pencil
Scissors
Yarn

To make a pompom

1 Copy the Pompom Template (p190) onto thick paper or card and cut out. You will need two.

2 Cut a 25cm (10 in.) length of yarn. Place one of your card pompom shapes down on your surface and lay the length of yarn along it, as shown. The ends of the yarn should overhang the card.

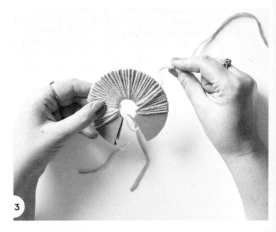

3 Place the second card pompom shape on top and carefully pick up both pieces, keeping the yarn sandwiched in between. Wrap both pieces with yarn, starting from one end and working back and forwards to cover the whole shape evenly about ten times.

4 Take the ends of the yarn sandwiched between the paper shapes, and tie them together, pulling tight to close up the gap in the middle. Slot the blade of a pair of scissors in between the two paper shapes, at one end, and cut, working all the way around. Hold everything together carefully.

5 Once you have cut all the way around, pull again on the two ends of the length of yarn to make a tighter knot.

6 Carefully remove the paper shapes. Trim the pompom to make it nice and smooth and round. You can attach a longer piece of wool to the knot if you need to hang it.

Note The template on p190 makes a pompom that is 10cm (4 in.). To make pompoms in different sizes, you will need to make your own version of the template – draw a larger or smaller outer circle, depending on the size you need. Then draw another smaller circle in the middle and cut out the bottom of the shape, copying the template. Remember that you will always lose around 1cm (¼ in.) of pompom while trimming the edges.

To make a tassel

1 Cut out a 12 x 10cm (4¾ x 4 in.) piece of thick paper or card.

2 Wrap the yarn around the piece of card lengthways, about ten times. The more times you wrap the yarn round, the thicker your tassel will be.

3 Cut two 20cm (8 in.) lengths of yarn. Take one of the lengths, and feed one end under the wrapped yarn, at the top edge of the paper. Tie a strong double knot.

4 Using scissors, cut the yarn along the bottom edge of the paper.

5 Holding the yarn together, take the second 20cm (8 in.) length of yarn and wrap it around the tassel, 3cm (1¼ in.) below the knot, as shown. Tie a double knot. To finish, trim the bottom edge of the tassel so the lengths of yarn are all even.

Note These instructions will make a tassel that is 11cm (4¾ in.). If you would like to make tassels in different sizes, cut a piece of card that is slightly larger than the desired size of the finished tassel. For example, for a 5cm (2 in.) tassel, cut a piece of card 6 x 10cm (2¼ x 4 in.).

Traditional
PAJĄKI

KALINKA PAJĄK

This is a small pająk, perfect for beginners. It has a basic structure decorated with classic Kalinka Pompoms. While making it I was inspired by the rich colours of Pierre Bonnard's paintings - inspiration can strike us anywhere, so I recommend looking around to find other great colour combinations.

Length 60cm (23½ in.) • **Width** 32cm (12½ in.)

What you will need

Rye or paper straw
Ruler
Scissors
Coloured card in six
  assorted colours
  (I used cream, peach,
  pale pink, red, fuchsia
  and burgundy)
3cm (1¼ in.) circle punch
  (optional)
Compass
Pencil

Tissue paper in red
  and fuchsia
30cm (12 in.) diameter
  metal hoop
Fuchsia crepe paper
Glue
Cotton crochet thread
Needle
5mm (¼ in.) ribbon

Before you start

Cut pieces of straw:
  56 x 3cm (1¼ in.)
  16 x 6cm (2¼ in.)

Cut card circles:
  64 x 3cm (1¼ in.) in
  assorted pinks and reds

**Prepare the layers for
a Kalinka Pompom (p38):**
  1 x 10cm (4 in.) in red

**Make Kalinka Pompoms
(pp38–39):**
  4 x 10cm (4 in.) in fuchsia

Tip I used six colours in my design as I like this gradient effect, but you can use fewer or many more colours, whatever you like! You also don't have to use a circle punch for the arms - try out different shapes.

Structure of the PAJĄK

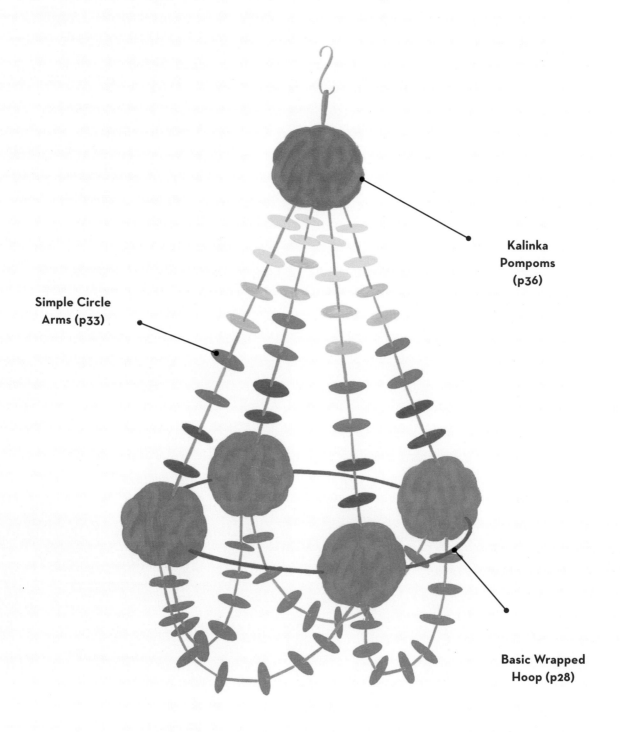

Kalinka Pompoms (p36)

Simple Circle Arms (p33)

Basic Wrapped Hoop (p28)

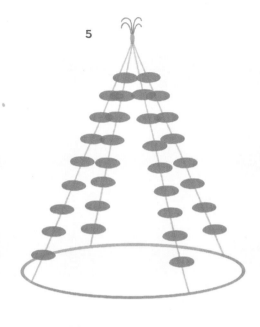

5

8

1 Wrap the hoop with the fuchsia crepe paper (p28).

Making the upper arms
2 Cut four 80cm (31½ in.) lengths of cotton thread. Attach them symmetrically to the hoop at the quarter points – wrap around the hoop and tie tightly, making at least two knots.

3 Take the first thread, thread the loose end onto a needle and then thread on a long straw, seven short ones, then another long one, with eight card circles in between.

Tip Hold the card circle between your fingers on both sides to keep it stable – it will be easier to thread the needle and make a hole. Otherwise, the paper will bend.

4 Continue to thread the remaining three arms. Gather the threads at the top and tie a strong double knot.

5 Lift up your structure and check if your pająk is hanging straight (the hoop should be level). If not, undo the knot, adjust the length of the arms and then make the knot again. Hang the structure to work on the lower parts.

Making the lower arms
6 Cut four 60cm (24 in.) lengths of thread. Wrap the first piece of thread around the hoop, where one of the upper arms is attached. Tie a double knot.

7 Thread a needle onto the loose end. Thread on a long straw, then seven short ones, then another long one, with eight card circles in between.

Tip Leave space between the hoop and the long straw so that the arms can dangle nicely.

8 Wrap the loose end of the dangling arm around the hoop, where the next upper arm is attached, making two knots. Continue threading the remaining three until you have attached all four dangling lower arms.

Attaching the pompoms

9 Cut a 60cm (23½ in.) length of thread, thread it with a needle, double it and secure the end with a double knot. Pull the needle through the top knot of the pająk structure twice, making sure the thread is securely attached to the knot.

10 Thread the 15 red layers of Kalinka Pompom onto the needle, changing the direction of the petals (one up, one down). Push the layers down the thread to form the pompom. Cut out a tiny square pad of tissue paper, thread it on to the needle and push it down to the middle.

11 Cut a 25cm (10 in.) length of ribbon, fold it in half and tie it at the bottom. Attach the ribbon to the middle of the pompom with one of the threads – take both pieces of thread and make a tight double knot on top of the ribbon. Cut off any excess threads.

12 Take the four fuchsia Kalinka Pompoms and attach each pompom tightly to the hoop between the lower and upper arms. Wrap one thread above the hoop, another one under the hoop. Pull both threads and make a double knot. Cut off any excess thread.

13 Once you have attached all the pompoms, if necessary, move the lower arms so they sit inside the pompoms. Fluff out all of the pompoms and move them around the hoop so the hoop is hidden by the pompoms.

10

12

SUNNY PAJĄK

This pajꜣk has an unusual shape – it reminds me of an old church bell. Unfortunately, this is not a very popular design these days. I've seen it just once in real life, otherwise only when looking through old books with archive photos. I would love to keep the design alive, so I've included my own version here.

Length 95cm (37½ in.) · **Width** 50cm (19½ in.)

What you will need

Rye or paper straw

Ruler

Scissors

3cm (1¼ in.) circle punch (optional)

Peach card

Compass

Pencil

Tissue paper in orange, peach, coral and yellow

Needle

Cotton crochet thread

Foil

2 x 35cm (13¾ in.) diameter metal hoops

Crepe paper in cream and yellow

Glue

5mm (¼ in.) ribbon

Before you start

Cut pieces of straw:
120 x 6cm (2¼ in.)
12 x 10cm (4 in.)

Cut card circles:
93 x 3cm (1¼ in.)
in peach

Prepare layers for Kalinka Pompoms (p38):
1 x 8cm (3¼ in.) in yellow
12 x 12cm (4¾ in.) in coral

Make Kalinka Pompoms (p38–39):
24 x 10cm (4 in.) – 12 in orange and 12 in peach

Structure of the PAJĄK

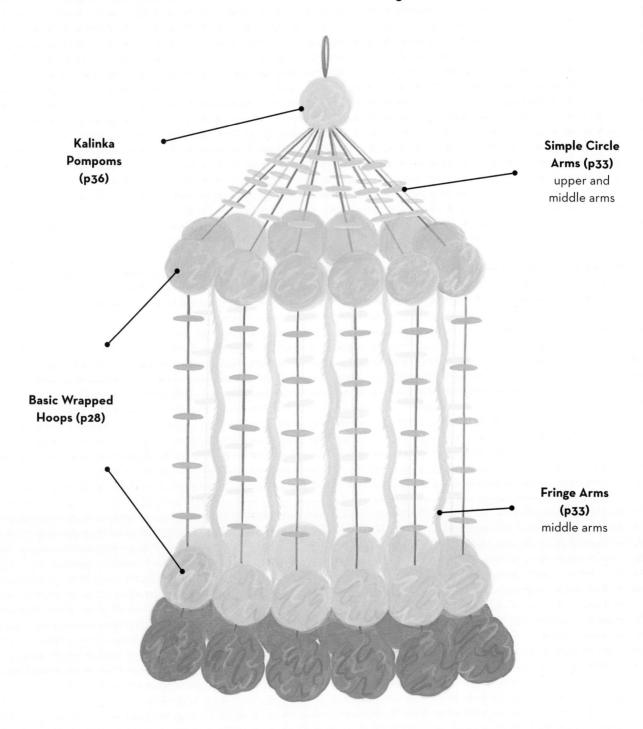

**Kalinka
Pompoms
(p36)**

**Simple Circle
Arms (p33)**
upper and
middle arms

**Basic Wrapped
Hoops (p28)**

**Fringe Arms
(p33)**
middle arms

1 Wrap both hoops in cream crepe paper (p28).

Making the upper arms
2 Cut 12 50cm (19½ in.) lengths of thread. Attach them symmetrically to one of the hoops. Start by attaching four threads at the quarter points, and then add two more in each gap, equal distances apart. Thread the needle through one of the loose ends and thread on four short pieces of straw with three card circles in between. Repeat with the remaining 11 arms.

3 Gather all the threads together at the top and make a double knot. Hang your structure and check that it hangs straight. If not, untie the knot and adjust the arms.

Making the top pompom
4 Gather the 15 layers for the 8cm (3¼ in.) yellow Kalinka Pompom. Cut a 30cm (12 in.) length of thread, thread onto a needle and make a knot in the end. Pull the needle through the top knot of the upper arms twice, so it's securely attached.

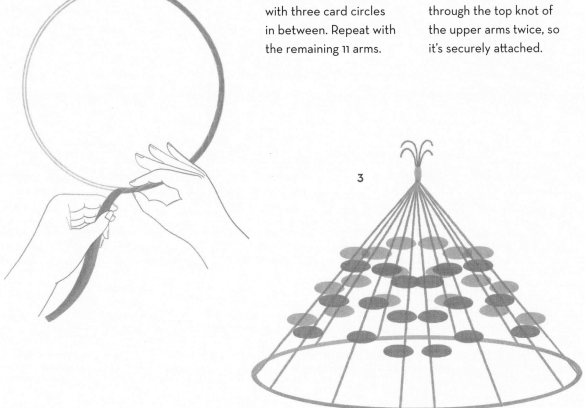

1

3

5 Thread all the yellow Kalinka layers onto the needle, changing the direction each time (one up, one down). Push the layers right down to the knot. Cut out a small square pad of tissue paper (7mm/¼ in.), with about eight layers). Thread this onto the needle and push it down inside the pompom. Cut off the needle and tie a double knot.

6 Cut a 25cm (10 in.) length of ribbon, fold it in half and tie it at the bottom. Tie the ribbon to the middle of the pompom with one of the threads. Trim off any excess threads.

Making the middle arms

7 Cut 12 x 60cm (23½ in.) lengths of thread and attach them to the same hoop at the points where the upper arms are tied.

8 Prepare the second wrapped hoop. Make four symmetrical marks on the hoop with a pencil at quarter points, and then add two more in each gap, equal distances apart. You should have a total of 12 marks, which match up to where the arms are tied onto the other hoop.

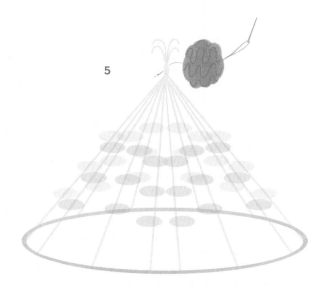

5

9 Start threading the first middle arm with six short pieces of straw with five card circles in between. You will need to attach the second hoop to the middle arms. I recommend that you start by threading four opposite arms first (the ones at the quarter points) and then attach the second hoop to these four by tying in place.

Tip To prevent straws falling off the threads while you are working on the other arms, you can loosely tie the ends temporarily to the upper hoop.

10 After the first four arms are attached to the bottom hoop, thread the remaining eight arms and tie them on, one by one.

11 To make the Fringe Arms, cut 12 45cm (17¾ in.) strips of yellow crepe paper, 3cm (1¼ in.) in width. Make 2cm (¾ in.) cuts all along one side, close together, to create the fringing. Glue the first strip to the upper hoop, in a gap between two of the threaded middle arms, twist it five times and glue the end to the bottom hoop. Continue with the rest of the arms. Trim off any excess paper if necessary.

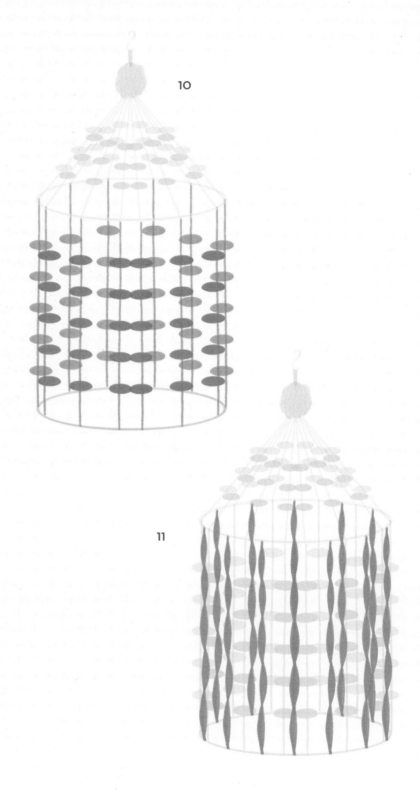

10

11

Attaching the pompoms

12 Gather together 15 of the layers for the 12cm (4¾ in.) coral Kalinka Pompoms, and thread them onto a 30cm (12 in.) thread with a foil covered knot at one end. Cut a small square piece of foil (7mm/¼ in.), wrap it around the thread and push it down inside the pompom so it stays round. Thread on one long piece of straw and then tie it to the bottom hoop, where one of the middle arms is attached. Make and attach the other coral pompoms the same way.

13 Take the completed 10cm (4 in.) Kalinka Pompoms and attach them to both hoops as shown. I used one colour for each hoop. Tie them to the hoops where the arms are attached. Hold one of the pompom threads above the hoop, with the second one under it, pull them tight and make a double knot. Trim off any excess thread.

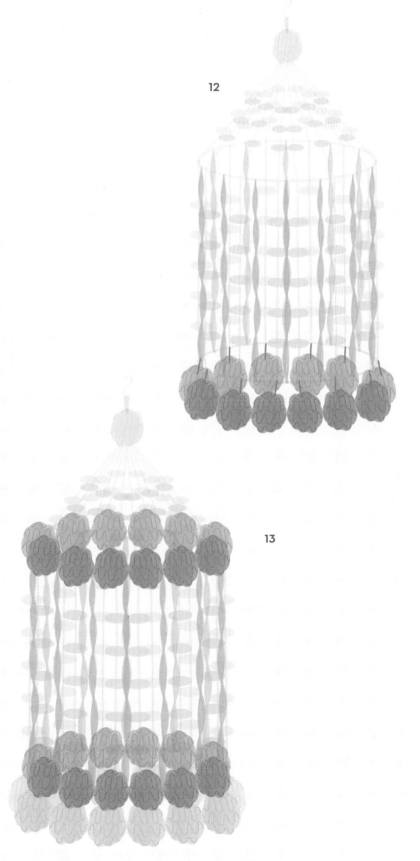

12

13

+ Helena +

I was born in Lublin, in the eastern part of Poland. On the outskirts of the city, near where I used to live, there is the Open Air Village Museum.

I remember my first visit to the museum, with its beautiful original wooden houses with amazing interiors and decorative objects. This is where I saw my first pająk. This unique, colourful decoration was hanging above a table in one of the whitewashed rooms.

Many years later I had the pleasure of meeting the woman behind the beautiful pająki in the museum.

Helena Półtorak is a proper pająki expert. She was also born in Lublin and has made pająki most of her life. She learned how to make them from her mother and then she honed her knowledge and skills while working in the Open Air Village Museum.

The number of different pająki designs she has made is remarkable. Looking through her archive of photographs was such an inspirational and unforgettable lesson for me. She remembers making a very old type of circular pająk, which had long rye straw pieces adorned with flowers that were stuck into a ball of dough and then hung. She was also highly skilled at producing a range of geometric and flowery pająki.

Helena taught me how to fold paper into tiny flowers, which are perfect for geometric pająki, and how to twist paper into thick garlands. It was she who introduced me to tiny pająki Christmas decorations. I had never seen anything like these before. Made with paper, rye straw and different types of beads, these are miniature versions of larger pająki. She remembers these were a must-have decoration for Christmas, but unfortunately they're now forgotten.

She also loved making other traditional Christmas decorations, such as paper angels and ballerinas dressed in traditional costumes. Today she has stopped making pająki and Christmas decorations due to health reasons. I am very happy I can include her designs in my book so they won't be lost.

GEOMETRIC PAJĄK

I would like to dedicate this pająk to Helena. During her career she created so many pająki and she generously shared her knowledge with me, including how to make beautiful paper carnations. This pająk is built from smaller geometric modules. Once you know how to build the basic structure you can add more modules and make it quite spectacular!

Length 50cm (19½ in.) • **Width** 50cm (19½ in.)

What you will need

Rye or paper straw
Ruler
Scissors
Tissue paper in teal
  and peach
Compass
Pencil
Needle
Cotton crochet thread
Foil
Pins
Foam board (around
  50cm/20 in. square)

Before you start

Cut pieces of straw:
  4 x 7cm (2¾ in.)
  48 x 10cm (4 in.)
  60 x 15cm (6 in.)

Make Carnation Flowers (p60):
  32 x 5cm (2 in.) diameter

Tip I used two colours for the flowers in my pająk – peach for the large structure and teal for the smaller ones. You can use as many colours as you like.

Structure of the PAJĄK

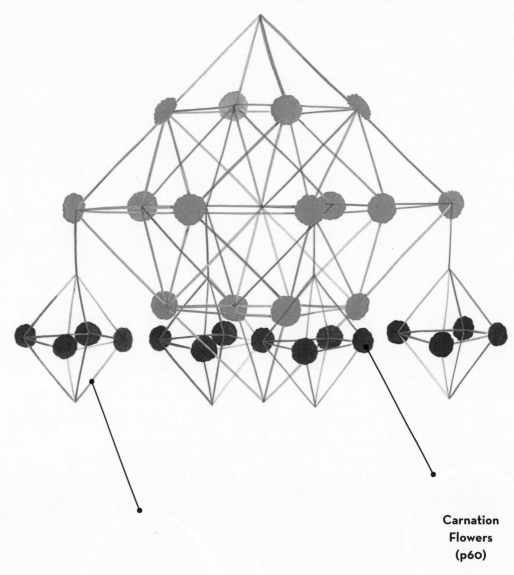

Rye straws

Carnation
Flowers
(p60)

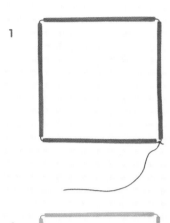

1

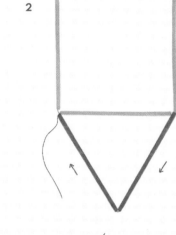

2

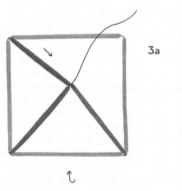

3a

3b

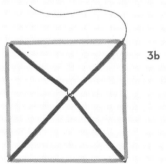

Making the first layer

1 You need to create the first layer of four pyramids using only the long (15cm/6 in.) pieces of straw. Cut a 1m (39 in.) length of thread and thread onto a needle. Thread on four pieces of straw, form them into a square shape and make a knot as shown. Pin each corner to a surface, for example a foam board, so it is easier to build the next layers.

2 Starting from the lower right corner of the square (where the knot is), thread on two more pieces of straw to create a triangle. Pull the needle under the thread in the lower left corner and make a knot so the triangle is secure.

3 Attach another 40cm (15¾ in.) length of thread to the top left corner and thread the needle onto the loose end. Thread on the first piece of straw, lift up the triangle from the other side and wrap the thread under the top of the triangle so it stays upright. Make a knot on top. Thread the next straw and then wrap it under the thread in the top right corner and make a knot. This is your pyramid module.

4 Using any excess thread from the first pyramid, thread three more straws to create another square. Then build a pyramid on top in the same way. If you run out of the thread, tie on another piece with a strong knot. Keep in mind that the length of the thread needs to be longer than all the straws you need to thread.

4

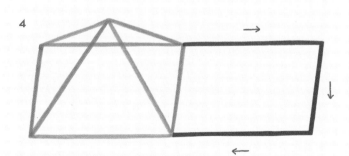

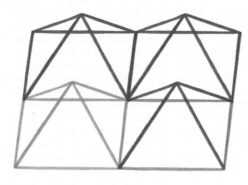

5

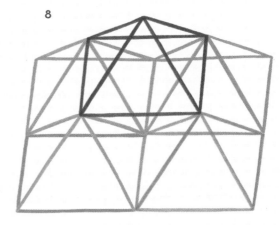

8

5 Continue to make two more modules in the same way, until you have four pyramids built for the first layer.

Making the top pyramid
6 Start building the next platform, the top pyramid. Attach an 80cm (31½ cm) length of thread to the top of the lower pyramid. Thread the needle and thread the first straw, still working with just the long (15cm/6 in.) straws. You need to create a square base for the top pyramid.

7 Place the straw between the top of another pyramid (top right), wrap the thread under the top and make a knot to secure it. Thread another two pieces of straw and place them between the remaining tops of the lower pyramid.

8 Then, build the top of the pyramid the same way you built the lower ones. Attach a 40cm (15¾ in.) length of thread to the lower right corner of the base, make a knot, thread the needle and thread two pieces of straw to create a triangle. Knot the thread to the lower left corner. Attach another 40cm (15¾ in.) length of thread to the opposite right top corner and thread first piece of straw. Wrap it under the top of the opposite triangle and make a knot so it stays upright. Thread another piece of straw and tie it to the top left corner. The first half of your pajak is ready.

9

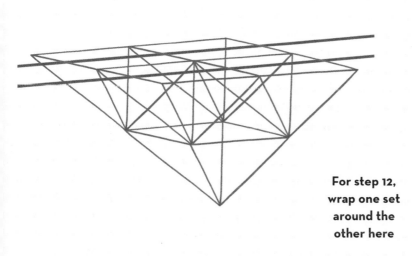

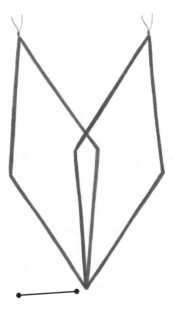

**For step 12,
wrap one set
around the
other here**

Completing
the second half

9 Now you need to flip over the half pyramid and add another two layers to finish the structure. Remove the pins so you can move it easily. The best way to complete the pająk is to suspend the structure on two long sticks and support them between higher objects such as chairs or piles of books so you can work easily on the top structure. The sticks should be under the straws of the bottom pyramid.

10 Follow the instructions from steps 2–8 to create two more layers. Once you have built the whole structure, cut 20cm (8 in.) of thread to make a loop, fold it in half and attach to the top of the pająk. Make a double knot and hide it at the bottom. You can now hang your pająk.

Making the
smaller modules

11 You need to build four smaller modules which will be attached to the four corners of the pająk. Use 10cm (4 in.) straw pieces. Each diamond shape is made of 12 pieces. Cut a 50cm (19½ in.) length of thread and thread four pieces of straw. Fold them in half and make a double knot. Repeat with another set of four pieces of straw. Before making the knot on the second set, wrap the thread with the previously prepared set so they are attached at the bottom. Make a double knot on top.

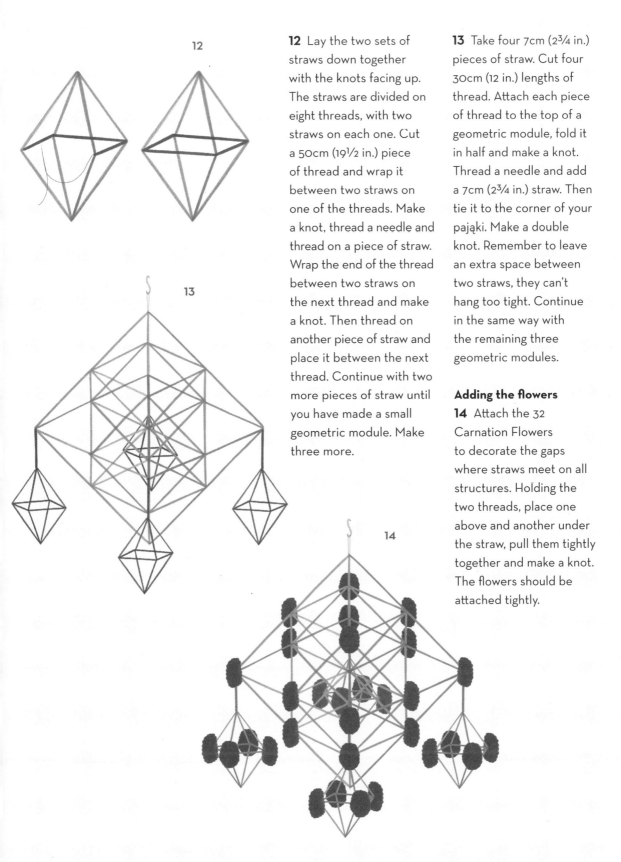

12 Lay the two sets of straws down together with the knots facing up. The straws are divided on eight threads, with two straws on each one. Cut a 50cm (19½ in.) piece of thread and wrap it between two straws on one of the threads. Make a knot, thread a needle and thread on a piece of straw. Wrap the end of the thread between two straws on the next thread and make a knot. Then thread on another piece of straw and place it between the next thread. Continue with two more pieces of straw until you have made a small geometric module. Make three more.

13 Take four 7cm (2¾ in.) pieces of straw. Cut four 30cm (12 in.) lengths of thread. Attach each piece of thread to the top of a geometric module, fold it in half and make a knot. Thread a needle and add a 7cm (2¾ in.) straw. Then tie it to the corner of your pajaki. Make a double knot. Remember to leave an extra space between two straws, they can't hang too tight. Continue in the same way with the remaining three geometric modules.

Adding the flowers
14 Attach the 32 Carnation Flowers to decorate the gaps where straws meet on all structures. Holding the two threads, place one above and another under the straw, pull them tightly together and make a knot. The flowers should be attached tightly.

PURPLE PAJĄK

If you're feeling confident, this is a more challenging version of the Kalinka Pająk project (p68). I love looking to the world of fashion for ideas and I was inspired by the colour combinations from Balenciaga's Spring Summer 2017 collection.

Length 80cm (31½ in.) • **Width** 45cm (17¾ in.)

What you will need

Rye or paper straw

Ruler

Scissors

3cm (1¼ in.) circle punch (optional)

Compass

Pencil

Coloured card in blue and purple

Tissue paper in blue, purple and brown

Two needles

Cotton crochet thread

Foil

35cm (13¾ in.) diameter metal hoop

Blue crepe paper

Glue

5mm (¼ in.) ribbon

Before you start

Cut pieces of straw:

159 x 3cm (1¼ in.)

59 x 6cm (2¼ in.)

4 x 8cm (3¼ in.)

Cut card circles:

212 x 3cm (1¼ in.)

in blue and purple

Prepare layers for Kalinka Pompoms (p38):

3 x 10cm (4 in.) in blue

4 x 10cm (4 in.) in brown

Make Kalinka Pompoms (pp38–39):

4 x 10cm (4 in.) in purple

Structure of the PAJĄK

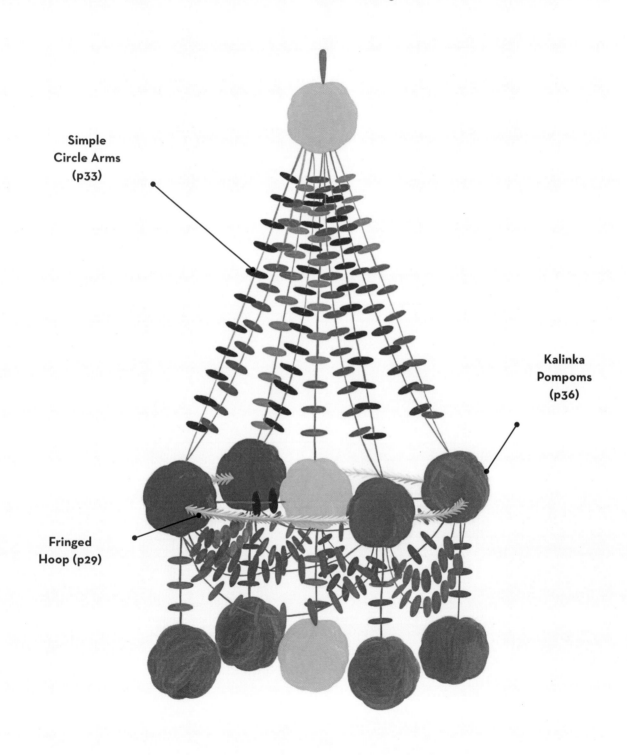

Simple
Circle Arms
(p33)

Kalinka
Pompoms
(p36)

Fringed
Hoop (p29)

1 Wrap the hoop in a fringe style with blue crepe paper (p29).

Making the crossed arms

2 Cut four 30cm (12 in.) lengths of thread. Attach them to the wrapped hoop at the quarter points with a double knot. Thread one arm with a medium (6cm/2¼ in.) straw, a card circle, a short (3cm/1¼ in.) straw, a card circle, then a long (8cm/ 3¼ in.) straw. Repeat with the opposite arm and join in the middle with a knot. Thread the other two arms and tie them all in place in the centre.

Making the inner upper arms

3 Cut four 80cm (31½ in.) pieces of cotton thread and attach them to the wrapped hoop where the crossed arms are. Thread each arm with one long (6cm/2¼ in.) straw, 11 short (3cm/1¼ in.) straws and finish with a long (6cm/ 2¼ in.), with 12 card circles in between the straws.

4 Repeat for the remaining three arms. Gather the arms at the top, and make a knot. Keep them on top of the middle crossed arms.

Making the outer upper arms

5 Cut four 70cm (27½ in.) lengths of cotton thread and attach them to the hoop in the same place as the other two sets of arms. Thread each one with one medium straw, ten short ones, and finish with another medium one, with 11 card circles in between.

6 Gather the two sets of opposite upper arms and knot them together. Attach a ribbon to the pająk structure temporarily and hang it to check if it hangs straight and to help you to work on the lower parts.

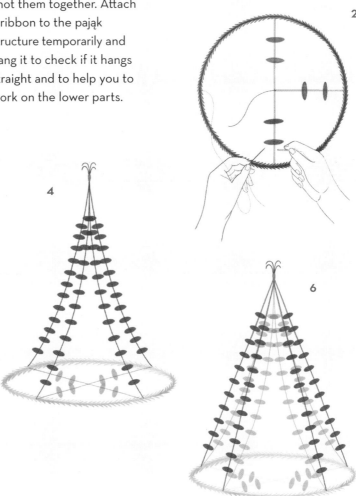

Making the middle arm

7 Gather together the 45 layers of tissue paper for the three blue central Kalinka Pompoms. Cut a very long piece of thread, about 1.8m (2 yd), thread a needle, fold the thread in half and tie a double knot in the end. Cut out a 2cm (¾ in.) square of foil and wrap it around the knot to create an almond-shaped 'stopper'.

8 Thread the first 15 layers of tissue paper onto the needle, through the centre of each piece, changing the direction of the petals (one facing up, one facing down), and push them down the thread. Cut off a 7mm (¼ in.) piece of foil, wrap it around the thread to create a ball and then push it down to the middle of the pompom and squeeze to give your pompom a nice, round shape.

9 Thread on a medium straw, two short ones and then another medium one, with a card circle in between each one.

10 Thread on a further seven layers of Kalinka Pompom, changing the directions of the petals once more. Pull the needle through the knot of the middle crossed arms twice so the arm stays in place. Do not cut off the needle, just put it to one side for now.

Making the lower dangling inner arms

11 Cut four 70cm (27½ in.) pieces of cotton thread for four dangling arms inside the pająk. Wrap and tie each arm to the hoop where the other arms are tied. Thread each arm with one medium straw, followed by six short ones, and finish with a final medium one. Add seven card circles in between the straws. Pull the needle through the middle 'half pompom', remove the needle and leave the thread on top of the middle crossed arms for now. Continue with the remaining three arms.

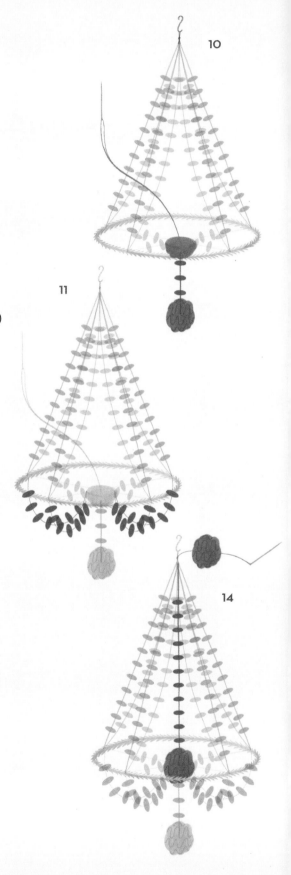

12 Once all four dangling arms are ready, gather all four threads (above the crossed middle arms). Check that the arms are even and then tie them all together. Don't tie them too tightly, they should dangle.

Finishing the middle arm
13 Take the long thread with the needle attached and thread the eight remaining layers of tissue paper to finish the pompom. Cut out a tiny square of foil (7mm/¼ in.), wrap it around the thread, push it down to the middle of the pompom and squeeze to give a nice, round shape. Thread a medium straw, followed by nine short ones and finish with another medium one, with ten card circles in between. Pull the needle through the top knot twice.

14 Thread the remaining 15 layers of tissue paper for the top pompom. Push them down to the knot, cut a small square pad of tissue paper as before, thread it and push inside the pompom. Cut the needle off and tie a double knot.

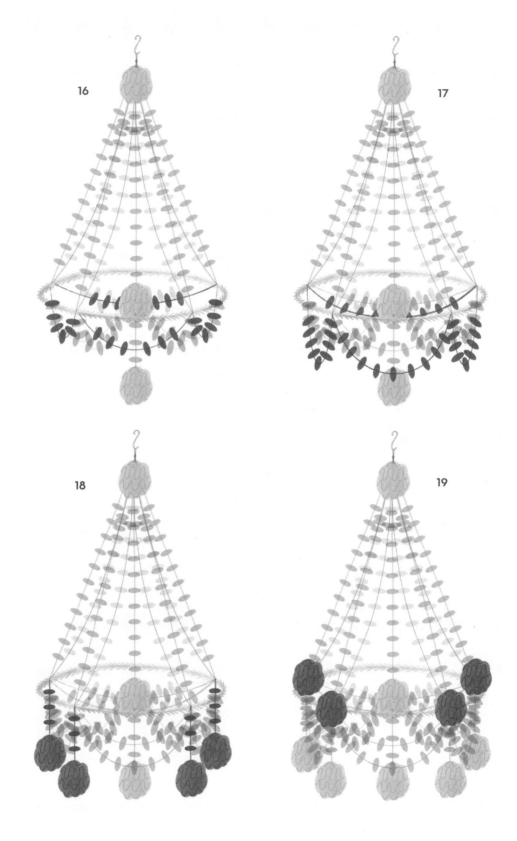

15 Cut 25cm (10cm) of ribbon, fold it in half and tie to create a loop to hang the pająk. Attach it inside the pompom by tying the threads in a strong double knot. The end of the ribbon should be hidden inside the pompom. Fluff out your pompom. Cut any excess threads. Hang your pająk again so you can finish the lower structure.

Making the lower outer dangling arms

16 Cut four 50cm (19½ in.) lengths of thread for four dangling arms. Wrap the first thread around the hoop, where one of the upper arms joins, make a knot and thread with a medium, five short and another medium straw with six card circles in between. Attach the end of the thread under the next upper arm, wrap it around the hoop and make a double knot. Continue with the remaining three arms.

17 Cut four 70cm (27½ in.) pieces of cotton thread for another set of lower dangling arms. Attach them under the shorter ones in the same way until you have wrapped them all around the hoop. Thread two long straws, eight short, and two long ones, with nine card circles in between.

Adding the remaining pompoms

18 Thread each of the four brown Kalinka Pompoms onto a 35cm (13¾ in.) thread. Once you have secured each pompom with a tiny foil ball, thread on a long straw, two short ones, then another long straw, with three card circles in between. Remove the needle and wrap the thread around the hoop. Make a single knot. Continue with the remaining three arms.

Once you have all your pompoms attached, check that they all hang at the same level. Then, make the final double knots.

19 Attach the last four purple Kalinka Pompoms to the hoop. Holding the two threads of the pompom, pull one above the hoop, another under and then tie tightly with a double knot. Cut the excess threads and arrange the pompoms so all the knots are hidden.

+ Zofia +

Lily, rose, poppy, peony or aster: there's no flower Zofia Samul can't recreate in paper.

She was born in a village in Kurpie, a beautiful region in north-east Poland surrounded by ancient forests. It's famous for its unique and rich folk art, which includes traditional wooden architecture, costumes, music, paper craft and Easter palms.

It also has its own regional dialect, hence the pająk is called *kierec* and is made of threaded peas adorned with Kurpie's traditional paper roses or other paper flowers. Here, a pająk refers to another paper decoration, one made of crepe paper strips attached to the ceiling in the middle of the room and then symmetrically pinned around the edge to create a large, star-shaped decoration above the floor.

When Zofia was a young girl she loved watching her grandmother and mother making paper cut-outs and other paper decorations. She smiles while talking about these memories from her childhood. She remembers the old traditional house they used to live in was always richly decorated for important celebrations like Christmas and Easter. All the walls had to be cleaned and whitewashed and then together they prepared different kinds of decorations: paper window curtains, circles and star paper cut-outs were stuck to the wall, a pająk was attached in the middle of the room, and a *kierec* would hang above the table.

This is a forgotten tradition nowadays, she adds sadly. Unfortunately, no one keeps the decorations anymore. For her, it's important to cultivate the tradition, so she's always happy to share her knowledge. She taught me how to fold paper to make a traditional Kurpie rose and how to make other flowers using a knife or wooden stick.

In the corner of her room she had arranged a saints' corner, or *święty kąt*, which used to be the most significant part of the countryside house. A crucifix or Madonna figurine would be placed in the centre of the table, between two symmetrical bouquets made of colourful paper flowers.

Zofia's KIEREC

This design, made with threaded peas and paper flowers, was inspired by my meetings with artist Zofia. She taught me how to make traditional paper roses – I have attached them here, in different colours, to the structure.

Length 67cm (26 in.) • **Width** 40cm (15¾ in.)

What you will need

Cotton crochet thread
Ruler
Scissors
Needle
Peas
Crepe paper in pale pink, peach, red, navy and green
Florist wire
Glue
Pencil
25cm (10 in.) diameter metal hoop
30cm (12 in.) diameter metal hoop
5mm (¼ in.) ribbon

Before you start

Thread 8 x 65cm (25½ in.) lengths of cotton threads with 45cm (17¾ in.) of peas (p33) and a gap at each end

Thread 1 x 2m (2¼ yd) length of cotton thread with peas

Thread 1 x 2.5m (2¾ yd) length of cotton thread with peas

Make Kurpie Roses (p54): 20, with stems

Tip Instead of peas, you can also use beads

Structure of the PAJĄK

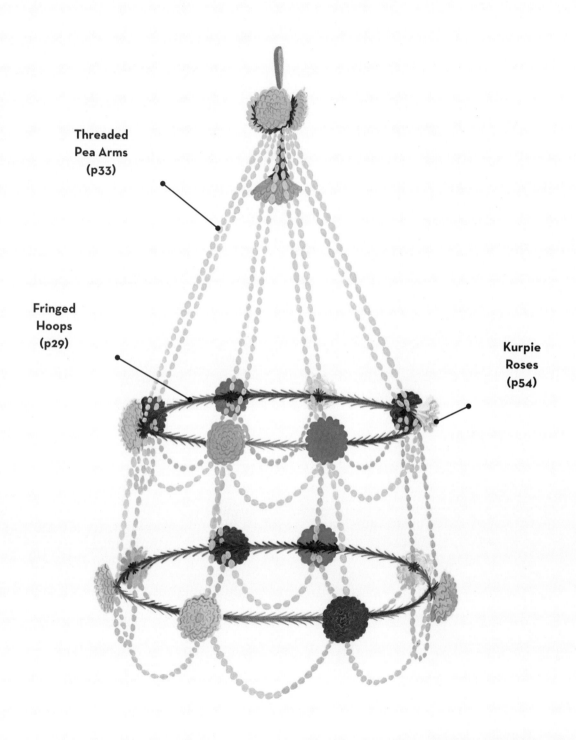

Threaded Pea Arms (p33)

Fringed Hoops (p29)

Kurpie Roses (p54)

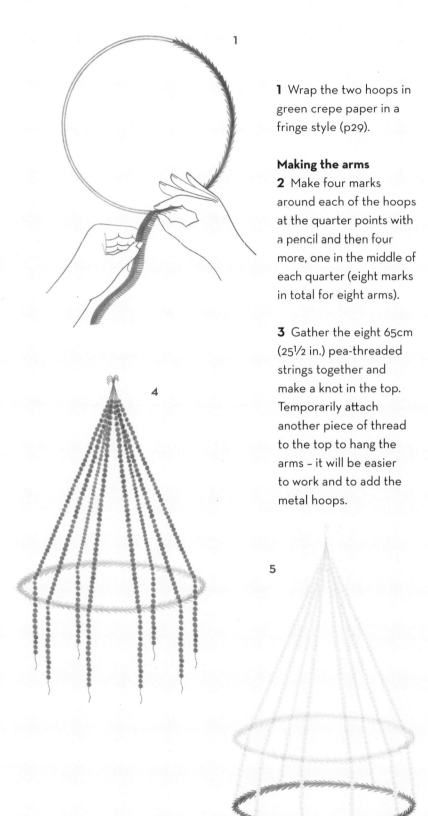

1 Wrap the two hoops in green crepe paper in a fringe style (p29).

Making the arms
2 Make four marks around each of the hoops at the quarter points with a pencil and then four more, one in the middle of each quarter (eight marks in total for eight arms).

3 Gather the eight 65cm (25½ in.) pea-threaded strings together and make a knot in the top. Temporarily attach another piece of thread to the top to hang the arms – it will be easier to work and to add the metal hoops.

4 Measure 30cm (12 in.) down from the top of each arm – this is the height you need to attach the 25cm (10 in.) hoop. Push the peas aside so that you have a gap in the string to wrap around the hoop. Attach four arms across the hoop at the marks at the quarter points. Wrap each arm around the hoop, and check if the hoop is attached straight. If not, you can move the peas and adjust the strings. Continue with the remaining four arms. If you like, you can glue them to the hoop so they won't move.

5 Next, attach the 30cm (12 in.) hoop at the bottom. Wrap each string round the hoop where the marks are and tie a double knot. Make sure the hoop hangs straight. Cut off any excess string.

Adding the waves

6 Attach the 2m (2¼ yd) pea-threaded string to the upper hoop where one of the arms is attached. Tie the end of the string around the hoop, then take the string over to where the next arm joins, creating a wave shape about 5cm (2 in.) deep, as shown. You don't need to make a knot each time you create a wave, just wrap it around the hoop. Attach the whole string around the hoop and then check each dangling wave is even. If so, push peas aside to make gaps in the string so it stays in place on the hoop. Make a knot and cut off any excess string.

7 Continue in the same way with the lower, longer 2.5m (2¾ yd) pea-threaded string and attach it to the bottom hoop. Each wave should be around 9cm (3½ in.) deep on that level. Don't worry if the waves looks a little bit messy and are moving around. You will attach roses on top of each one to secure them in place.

8 Cut a 25cm (10cm) length of ribbon, fold it in half, wrap it around the top knot and tie up at the bottom. Cut off any excess threads at the knot.

Attaching the roses

9 Place one of the Kurpie Roses under the knot, among the end of the threaded arms. Wrap the stem of the rose around the top knot so it is hanging down, as shown. Then, wrap three more Kurpie Roses around the knot and ribbon. They look beautiful on top of the structure as well as hiding the knot.

10 To finish, add the remaining sixteen Kurpie Roses to the hoop where arms are attached. Hold each Kurpie Rose close to the hoop and wrap the wire stem tight around the hoop.

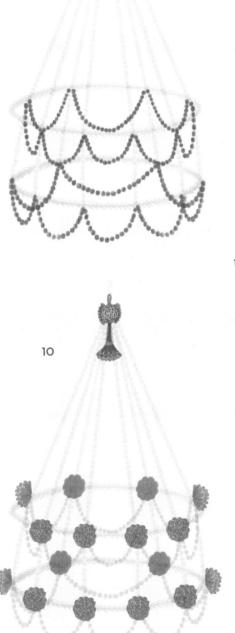

6

10

Łowicz PAJĄK

The Łowicz pająk is famous for its handwoven, octagonal woollen platform. I especially like the unique, flowery-like Tube Pompoms in this design.

Length 78cm (30¾ in.) • **Width** 35cm (13¾ in.)

What you will need

Rye or paper straw
Ruler
Scissors
Tissue paper in pale yellow, pale pink,
  grey, teal, white, pale brown and
  dark brown
Compass
Pencil
Pencil sharpener
Two needles
Glue
Foil
Cotton crochet thread
Spoon with a very flat, simple handle
3 x 45cm (18 in.) wooden dowel rods,
  3–4mm (⅛ in.) thick
Wool yarn in brown and pale pink
Pliers
5mm (¼ in.) ribbon

Before you start

Cut pieces of straw:
  219 x 3cm (1¼ in.)
  76 x 6cm (2¼ in.)

Cut Łowicz Circles (p33):
  281 x 3cm (1¼ in.) in white,
  pale pink, pale brown, dark
  brown and orange

Prepare the layers for Hedgehog Pompoms (p42):
  7 x 10cm (4 in.), six in teal,
  one in grey

Prepare the layers for Tube Pompoms (p48):
  2 x 8cm (3¼ in.) in grey

Make Tube Łowicz Pompoms (p50):
  6 x 8cm (3¼ in.) and 5cm (2 in.)
  diameter circles in yellow

Structure of the PAJĄK

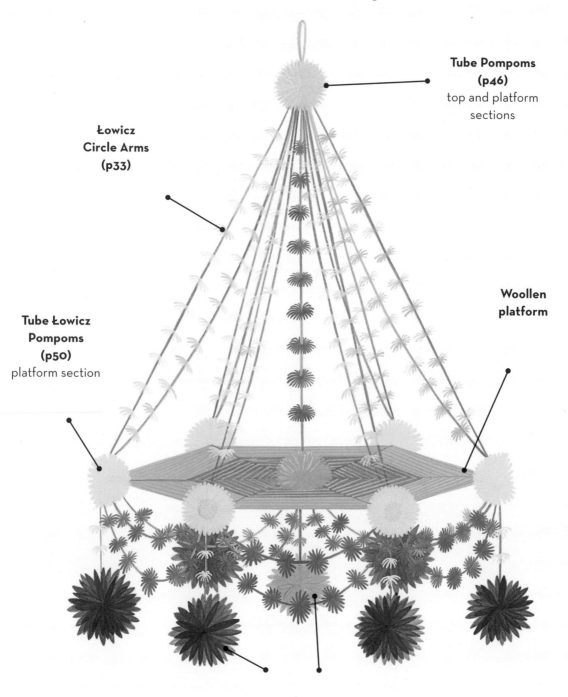

**Tube Pompoms
(p46)**
top and platform
sections

**Łowicz
Circle Arms
(p33)**

**Woollen
platform**

**Tube Łowicz
Pompoms
(p50)**
platform section

**Hedgehog
Pompoms
(p40)**
lower arms

Making the platform

1 Take the three dowel rods and mark the middle of each with a pencil. Cut 30cm (12 in.) of cotton thread, wrap it around the centre point of one of the dowels and make a tight knot. Now hold all three together and wrap around the middle a couple of times. Spread them out to form a six-armed star shape and start wrapping the thread around each dowel, going over then under. They will move about at the beginning – hold them tightly in position. Check they are all centred, adjust if not. Keep wrapping until you have around 1cm (½ in.) of thread and they are firmly in position.

2 Choose your yarn colours. Traditionally these are very colourful, but my design is more monochrome and I chose only two colours. Note that the first colour of your platform will be partly hidden, under the central pompom. Starting with your first colour, wrap the end of the yarn around one of the dowels, push it to the centre, and make a knot. Start wrapping each dowel with the yarn.

Keep going in the same direction – start wrapping from above one dowel, then wrap under and over again. This will give you a nice, flat colourful surface. The yarn can't be too loose, try to wrap it nice and firmly. You are aiming to create a flat platform.

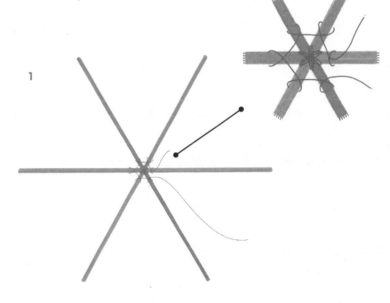

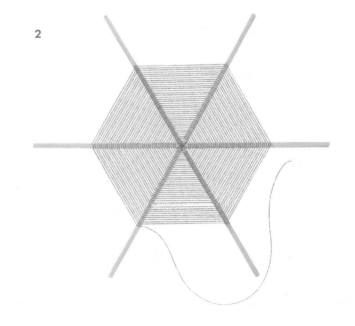

3 When you want to
change the colour of the
yarn, cut it off, wrap it
around one of the dowels
and make a knot. Take
another colour of yarn,
wrap it around the dowel
and carry on wrapping
around your platform.
Continue with the rest of
the colours until the whole
platform is covered. Do not
wrap right to the ends of
the dowels, leave a space
of 1.5cm (½ in.) uncovered.
Trim the dowels with pliers
if any are looking too long.

Note The side of the
platform with all the
knots (the top one) will
be hidden, which means
that while working on your
pająk later and attaching
the upper arms it should
be facing you. The 'right
side' of the platform will
be the one facing down.
That's because when you
hang your pająki high up,
you will see it from below.

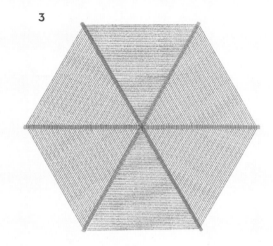

3

**Making the inner
upper arms**
4 Cut six 90cm (35½ in.)
lengths of thread. Wrap
a thread around the end
of one of the dowels and
make a knot. Thread a
needle and then thread it
onto a long straw followed
by 12 short ones with
13 paper Łowicz circles
in between. Finish with
another long straw. Repeat
with the remaining five
arms. When you have
finished, gather them
together and make
a knot. Lay them
on the platform.

4

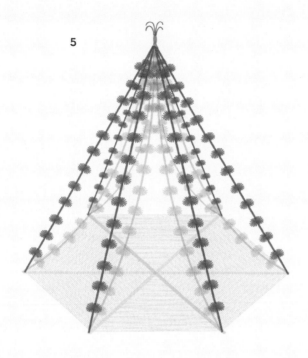

5

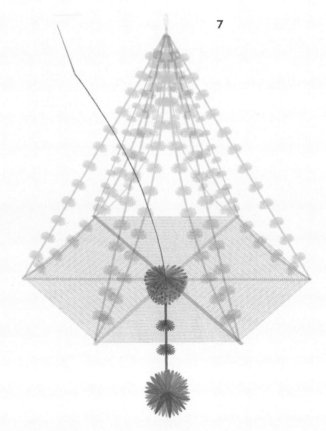

7

Making the outer upper arms

5 Cut six more 80cm (31½ in.) lengths of thread. Attach them to the platform at the same points that the other arms are attached. Thread a long straw, then 11 short ones, finishing with a long one and adding 12 paper Łowicz circles in between. Once you have threaded all the arms, gather them together and make a strong knot at the top. Gather the two sets of upper arms together and make a knot. The inside upper arms should be longer; they will fill up the upper part nicely, adding extra texture. Lift your pająk structure and check if it hangs straight. If necessary, re-adjust the arms. Hang your pająk so you can work on the lower parts.

Making the middle arm

6 Gather together the 12 layers for one of the Hedgehog Pompoms. Cut a 2m (2¼ yd) length of thread, fold in half and make a double knot. Cut out a square piece of foil (1cm/½ in.) and wrap it around the knot. Squeeze it tight to create an almond shape. Thread all 12 layers of Hedgehog Pompom on to the thread, pushing them down to the foil ball. Cut a second small square piece of foil (7mm/¼ in.), wrap it around the thread and push it down to the middle of the pompom. Squeeze it tight so it stays in place and helps the pompom to keep a nice, round shape.

7 Thread a long piece of straw onto the pompom thread, then a short one and then another long one, adding two Łowicz paper circles in between. Gather together 15 layers for one of the Tube Pompoms, and pull the needle through the centre of all the layers. Pull the needle through the middle of your platform and to secure it, pull it again through the top wool surface.

Tip Don't cut off the needle, you will need it later. Make sure that the arm has enough space and it's loose. It can't be attached too tightly, it needs to dangle easily.

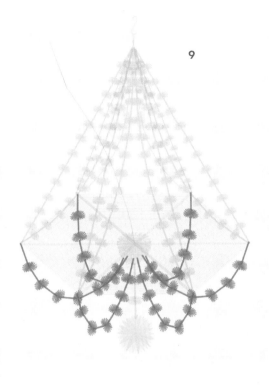

9

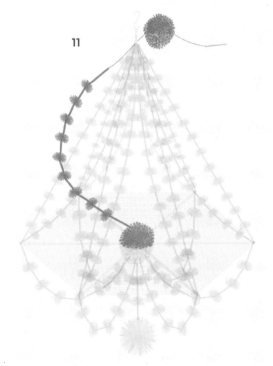

11

Making the inner lower dangling arms

8 Cut six 50cm (19½ in.) lengths of thread. Attach one of the threads to the end of one of the dowels, thread the needle and then thread on one long straw, six short ones and finish with another long one. Attach seven Łowicz paper circles between.

9 Pull the needle through the middle of the middle pompom into the woollen platform, leave it on one side, remove the needle and continue with the rest of the arms. Once you have attached and threaded all the arms through the platform, gather the ends together and make a knot. Cut off any excess thread. Remember not to tie them too tight, they should dangle easily.

Finishing the middle arm

10 Take the long thread you put to one side earlier and finish the middle tube pompom by adding the remaining 15 layers of tissue paper. Cut a small piece of foil, wrap it around the thread, push it down into the pompom and squeeze it into a ball. Thread the rest of the straw and circles, starting with a long one, then eight short ones, finishing with long one, with nine paper Łowicz circles in between. Pull the needle twice through the top knot (where the upper arms are joined) so it is securely attached.

11 Attach the top pompom by threading 30 layers of tissue paper for the remaining Tube Pompom and pushing them down to the knot. Cut out a tiny square pad of tissue paper (7mm/¼ in.), thread it and push it down to the middle of the pompom. Cut a 25cm (10 in.) piece of ribbon, fold it in half and tie it at the bottom. Attach the ribbon to the pompom. Take both pieces of thread and make a tight double knot on top of the ribbon. Cut off any excess threads. Hang the structure to work on the lower parts.

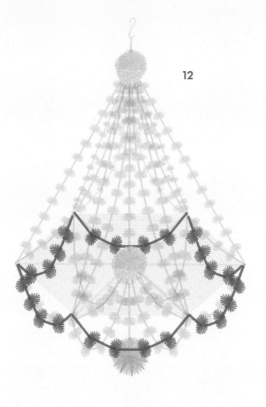

12

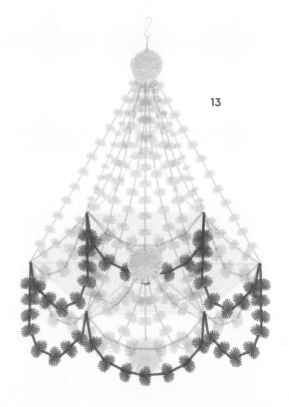

13

Making the outer dangling lower arms

12 Cut six 40cm (15¾ in.) lengths of thread. Attach the first thread to the end of the wool platform, winding it around one of the dowels and making a double knot. Thread with a long straw, then three short ones and finish with a long one. Add four paper Łowicz circles in between. Attach the end of the thread to the next dowel. Continue with the remaining five arms, all the way around.

13 Now cut six 50cm (19½ in.) lengths of thread for the longer dangling arms. Attach the six longer dangling arms under the shorter ones the same way as shorter ones. Each arm has two long straws (the first one and the last one), six short straws, and seven Łowicz circles in between. Attach them under the shorter arms.

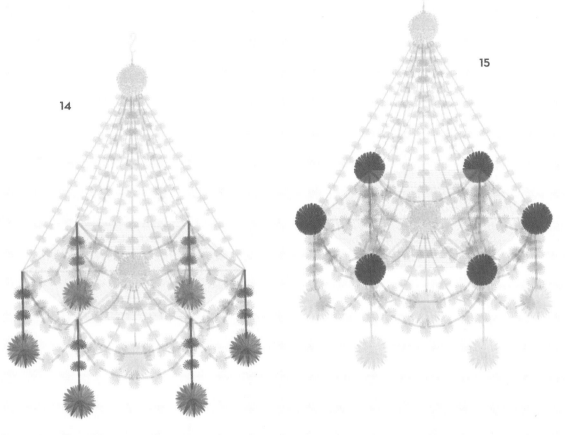

14

15

Attaching the
lower pompoms

14 Thread each of the six blue Hedgehog Pompoms onto a 35cm (13¾ in.) thread. Once you have secured each pompom with a tiny foil ball, thread a long straw, a short one, and another long one with two paper Łowicz circles in between. Remove the needle, wrap the thread around the dowel through the woollen platform. Make a single knot. Make sure there's a 0.5cm (¼ in.) gap between the dowel and the end of the long straw so the lower arm is not hanging too tightly. Attach the rest of the lower pompoms in the same way. Check if they're hanging straight and then make the second knot on each thread. Cut off the excess thread.

15 Attach each of the Łowicz Tube Pompoms to the ends of the dowel by pulling both threads through the edge of the woollen platform, one thread above and another under, and making a double knot. The pompoms should be attached tightly to the platform. Cut off any excess thread.

MASTER PAJĄK

This pajączk is a celebration of everything that you have learned in the book so far! Its large-scale features include beautiful fringe arms and an interesting diamond-detailed structure.

Length 125cm (49¼ in.) · **Width** 65cm (25½ in.)

What you will need

Rye or paper straw
Ruler
Scissors
Tissue paper in grey, white, black, pink and mustard
Compass
Pencil
Two needles
Spoon with a very flat, simple handle
Cotton crochet thread
Foil
50cm (19½ in.) metal hoop
Crepe paper in pale pink and blue
Glue
5mm (¼ in.) ribbon

Before you start

Cut pieces of straw:
156 x 3cm (1¼ in.)
16 x 6cm (2¼ in.)
28 x 8cm (3¼ in.)
32 x 20cm (8 in.)

Prepare layers for Tube Pompoms (p48):
11 x 8cm (3¼ in.)
1 in grey, 2 in white, 8 in black

Make 8cm (3¼ in.) Tube Pompoms (pp48–49):
8 with 30 layers in pink
8 with 20 layers in mustard

Make Fluffy Circles (p33):
174 sets (10 layers each)

Structure of the PAJĄK

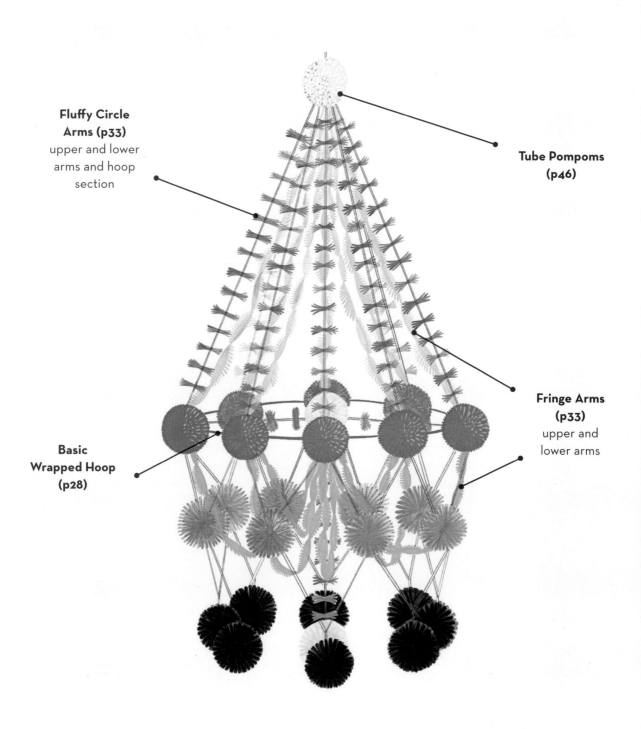

**Fluffy Circle
Arms (p33)**
upper and lower
arms and hoop
section

**Tube Pompoms
(p46)**

**Basic
Wrapped Hoop
(p28)**

**Fringe Arms
(p33)**
upper and
lower arms

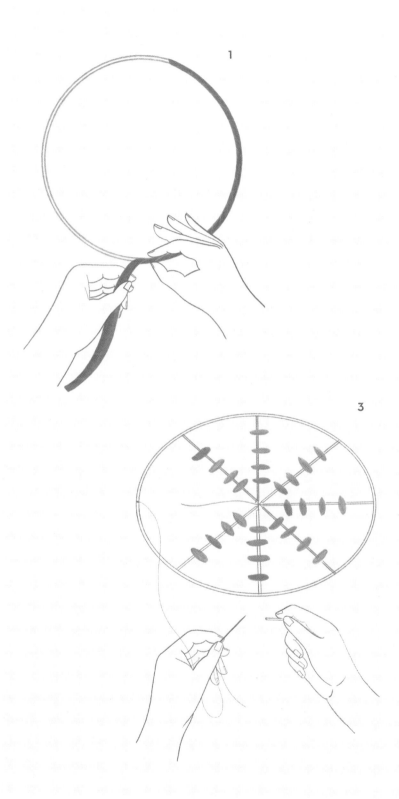

1 Wrap the hoop with pink crepe paper (p28).

Making the cross arms
2 Cut eight 45cm (17¾ in.) lengths of thread. Attach them to the hoop, at the quarter points, and then one in the middle of each quarter, making double knots. Thread each arm with one 8cm (3¼ in.) straw, followed by three short ones (3cm/1¼ in.), with four sets of Fluffy Circles in between, then finish with a 6cm (2¼ in.) straw.

3 Gather the loose ends of the arms together and tie them; tie two opposite threads in the middle at a time. Once you have tied all three pairs, tie them all together with one knot.

Making the upper arms

4 Cut eight 80cm (31½ in.) lengths of thread, and attach to the hoop where the cross arms are joined. Thread the needle onto one of the loose ends and start with an 8cm (3¼ in.) straw, then 14 short ones (3cm/ 1¼ in.), with 15 sets of Fluffy Circles in between. Finish with an 8cm (3¼ in.) piece. When all the arms are threaded, gather them together at the top and make a knot. Hang the structure to check if it's straight. If not, adjust and then make a second knot to secure.

Adding the upper fringes

5 Make eight 65cm (25½ in.) pale pink Fringe Arms (p33). Glue one end of each strip to the hoop where the arms are attached and twist each strip six times. Work in two groups: take the first four strips (attached at the quarter points) first and glue together at the top, then another four.

6 Cut a 30cm (12 in.) length of thread, thread onto a needle, fold in half and make a double knot. Hold the two sets of Fringe Arms, pull the needle through them and then through the top knot. The fringes should fill the middle space of your structure. Pull the needle again through the top knot to secure. Cut off the needle and tie a double knot. Cut off any excess thread. Hang your pająk to work on the lower parts.

Making the central arm

7 Gather together 90 layers for three Tube Pompoms (two in white and one in grey). Cut a 2.5m (2¾ yd) length of thread, thread the needle, fold it in half and make a strong double knot at the bottom. Cut a 2cm (¾ in.) foil square, and squeeze it into a ball around the knot. Don't cut off the needle, leave it to one side.

8 Thread 30 white Tube Pompom layers, pushing them down to the knot. Cut a tiny foil square (1cm/ ½ in.), wrap it around the thread and push into the middle of the pompom. Squeeze it into a tiny ball to help the pompom keep a nice round shape. Thread an 8cm (3¼ in.) straw, followed by eight short ones, with nine sets of Fluffy Circles in between. Finish with an 8cm (3¼ in.)straw. Thread on 15 layers of the white Tube Pompom. Pull the needle through the knot in the middle of the hoop twice, to secure.

Adding the bottom fringes

9 Make eight 60cm (23½ in.) blue Fringe Arms (p33). Glue one end of each strip to the hoop, where the upper arms are attached, twist each strip five times and glue the end of each arm inside the middle of the central Tube Pompom.

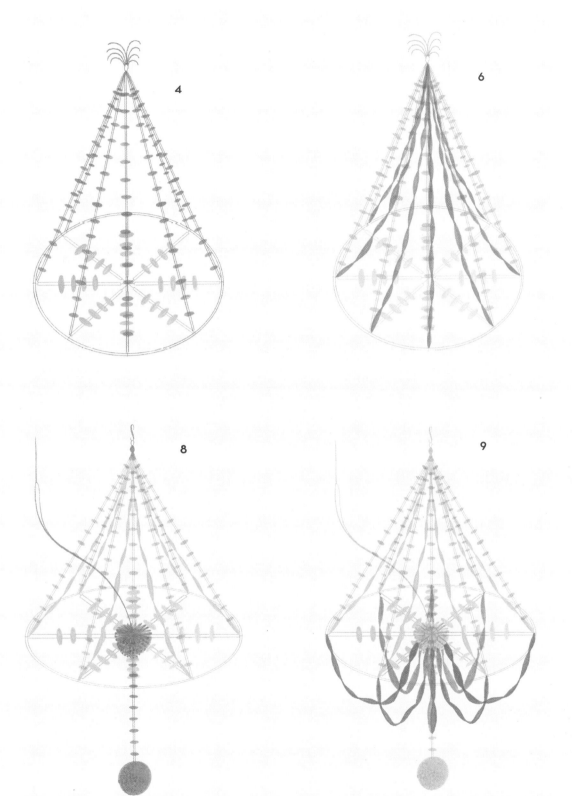

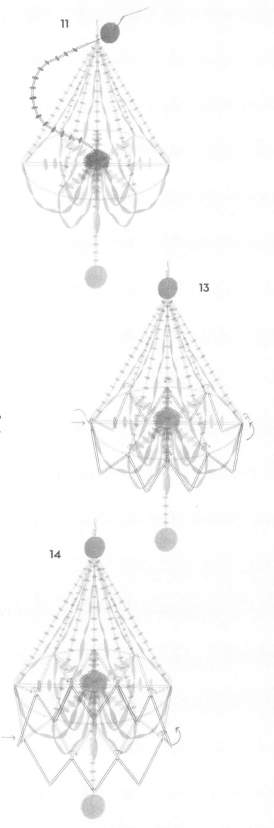

Finishing the central arm

10 Thread the rest of the 15 Tube Pompom layers onto the needle. Cut a foil square (1cm/½ in.), wrap it around the thread and push it down into the middle of the pompom. Finish threading the middle arm, starting with a long straw 8cm (3¼ in.), then 12 short ones with 13 sets of Fluffy Circles in between, and finish with a long straw. Pull the needle twice through the top knot, making sure the arm is not too tight.

11 Thread the 30 layers of grey tissue paper onto the needle and push it down to the knot. Cut a small (7mm/¼ in.) pad of tissue paper (about 8–10 layers), thread it and push it in the middle of the pompom. Cut off the needle and make a tight double knot.

12 Cut a 30cm (12 in.) length of ribbon, fold it in half and tie at the bottom. Push it down inside the pompom. Holding the two pompom threads, make a strong double knot on top through the ribbon. Cut off any excess thread. Hang your pająk.

Making the side structure

13 The side structure is made up of the longest 20cm (8 in.) pieces of straw. Cut a 70cm (27½ in.) piece of thread. Wrap the end onto the hoop where one of the upper arms meets the hoop. Thread a needle, then thread on two of the straws, wrap the thread under the next upper arm and make a knot. The two straws should create a triangle. Continue with the rest of the pieces of straw until there's a straw 'skirt' all around the hoop. (If you run out of thread, tie on another piece.)

14 Cut another 50cm (19½ in.) length of thread and attach it between two of the straws at the bottom of one of the triangles and make another straw skirt layer around the whole pająk.

Adding the pompoms

15 Gather together the black Tube Pompom layers. Cut eight 40cm (15¾ in.) lengths of thread. Wrap one of the threads between two straws on one of the lower triangles. Fold it in half and make a knot, thread a needle, thread on a 6cm (2¼ in.) piece of straw, and then 30 of the Tube Pompom layers. Cut out a small pad of tissue paper, as before. Thread it on and push it inside the pompom. Remove the needle and tie a double knot to secure. Continue with the remaining seven lower hanging pompoms in the same way. Make sure they're not attached too tightly. There should a space between the skirt and the lower straw so the pompoms can dangle easily.

16 Attach the eight mustard 20-layer Tube Pompoms to the middle of the straw skirt, between the top and lower triangles. Pull one thread above the straw and another under and then make a tight knot at the back of the pompom.

17 Attach eight final pink Tube Pompoms to the hoop, where the upper and lower arms meet. Pull one thread above the hoop and another under and then make a tight knot at the back of the pompom. Cut off any excess thread.

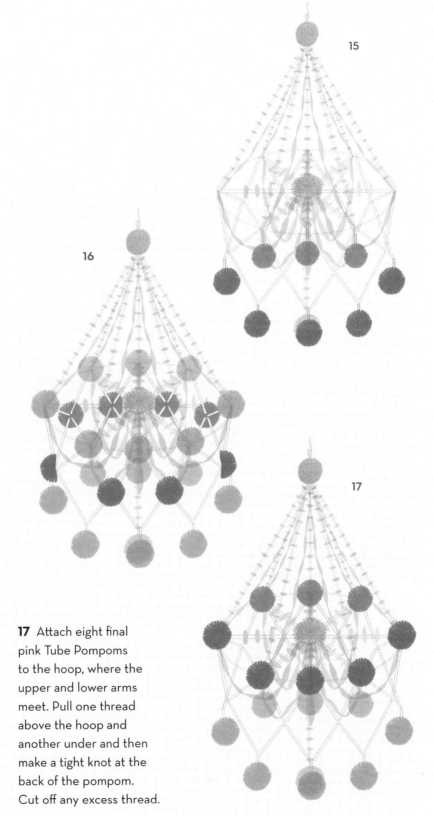

Contemporary
PAJĄKI

HABERDASHERY MOBILE

I love visiting haberdasheries, you can always find beautiful trims, sequins, flowers, tassels and much more! This pająk is for someone who thinks 'I can't make that'. You can make this design in less than an hour! I think fringe upholstery trim and oversized silk flowers give it such a unique look. You can also use any other treasures you find in your local haberdashery. It's a beautiful, elegant decoration for your bedroom or living room or even for a wedding!

Length 40cm (15¾ in.) • **Width** 30cm (12 in.) + flowers!

What you will need

30cm (12 in.) diameter brass hoop
Pencil
2cm (¾ in.) ric rac trim
Scissors
Glue
1.5m (1¾ yd) upholstery trim (mine had a
    10cm/4 in. fringe)
Florist wire
5 x silk flowers of your choice (I used
    oversized flowers, approx. 15cm/6 in.)

Tip This pająk works really well with an eclectic mixture of trims and flowers, so have a look in your local haberdashery and see what you can find!

Structure of the PAJĄK

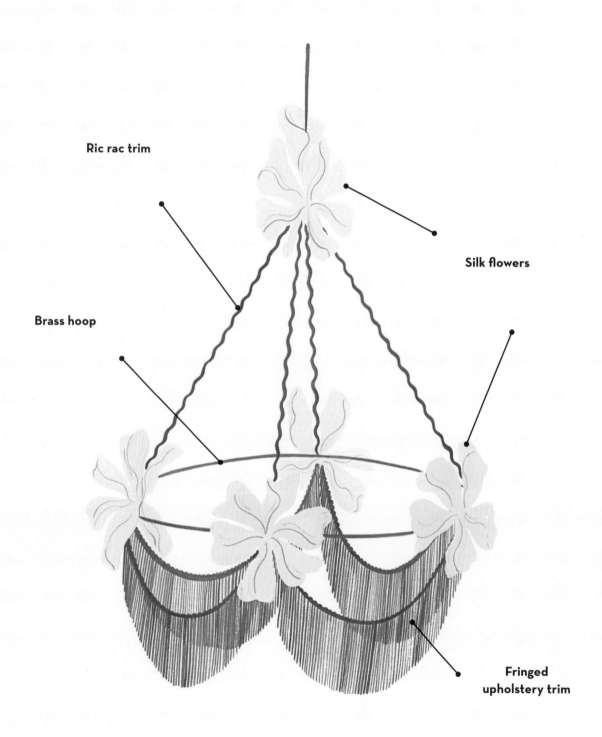

Ric rac trim

Silk flowers

Brass hoop

Fringed
upholstery trim

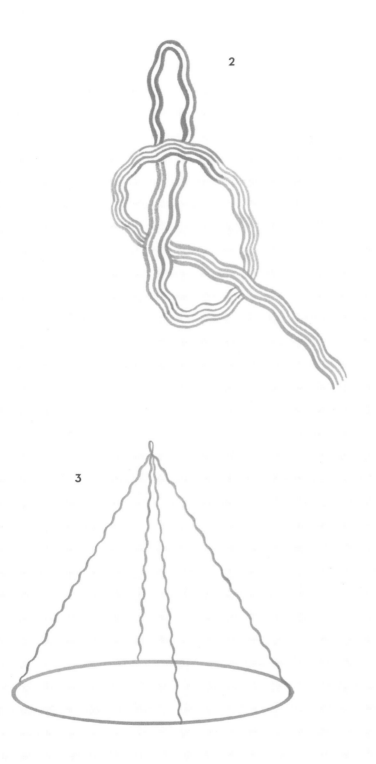

1 Prepare the brass hoop by making four symmetrical pencil marks, at the quarter points.

Making the upper arms
2 Cut two 70cm (27½ in.) lengths of ric rac trim. Hold the pieces together. Fold in half, and create a loop by making a strong knot about 3cm (1¼ in.) under the fold, to create the four arms. Make sure all the arms are the same length.

3 Attach the end of each arm to the hoop, where the marks are. Wrap the ric rac around the hoop, apply some glue and hold it tight to secure it. Hang the hoop to make the next stages easier.

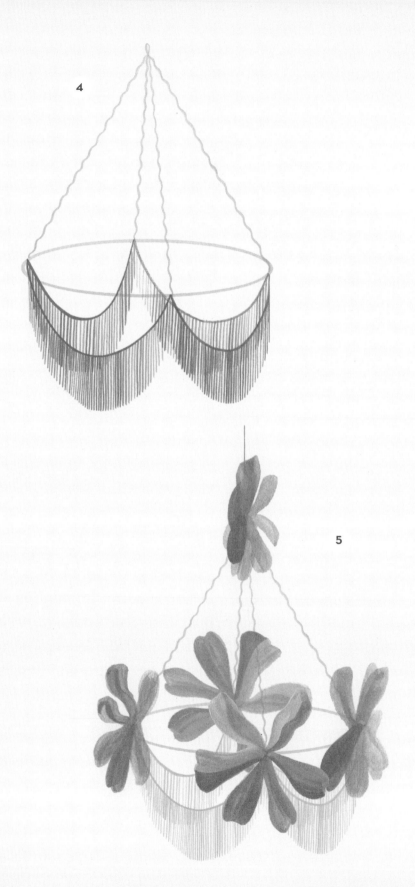

Making the lower hanging arms

4 Attach one end of the length of fringe trim under the one of the upper arms. To do this, pull through a short 2cm (¾ in.) piece of florist wire through the edge of the trim and then wrap it around the hoop. Attach the rest of the hanging arms in the same way. Check that they are all hanging down to the same level.

5 Finally, add the silk flowers – one to the top knot and four to the hoop, at the points where the upper and lower hanging arms meet. You can attach them securely with short pieces of florist wire.

MINI CHRISTMAS BAUBLE

Helena showed me how to make these tiny versions of pająki! They used to be popular Christmas tree decorations, but now sadly the tradition is dying out. In the past, families gathered together to make different types of decorations at Christmas time, so let's bring the tradition alive again and decorate our trees with these lovely mini pająki!

Length 15cm (6 in.) • **Width** 7cm (2¾ in.)

What you will need

Rye or paper straw

Ruler

Scissors

Tissue paper

Compass

Pencil

Needle

Cotton crochet thread

Foil

Coloured card

26 coloured beads,
   around 4–5mm (¼ in.)

Before you start

Cut pieces of straw:
   25 x 3cm (1¼ in.)

Prepare layers for a Carnation Flower (p60):
   20 layers of 4cm (1½ in.)

Structure of the PAJĄK

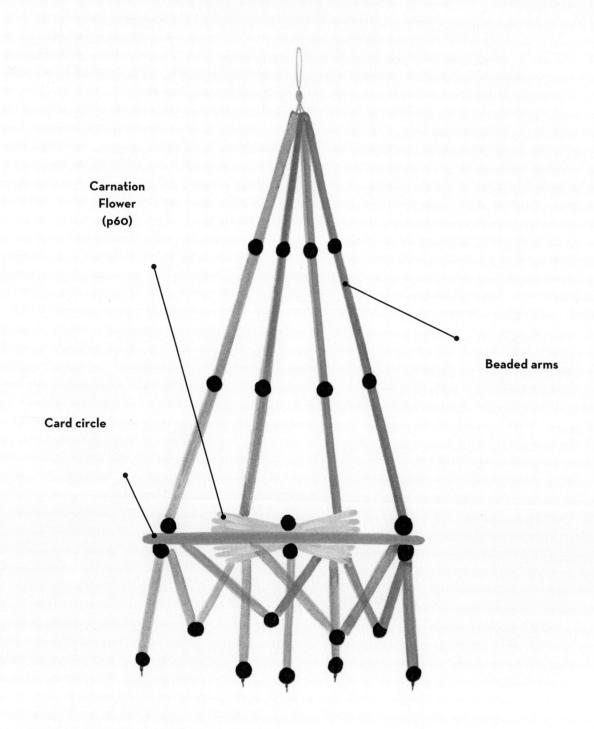

Carnation Flower (p60)

Beaded arms

Card circle

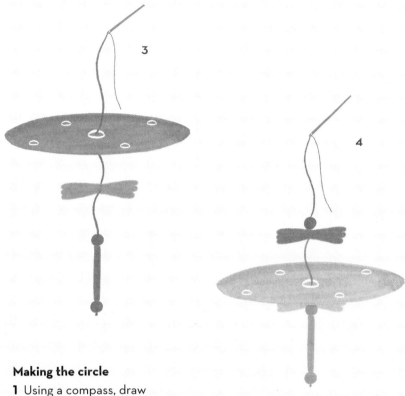

Making the circle

1 Using a compass, draw a 7cm (2¾ in.) circle on a piece of coloured card and cut it out. With a needle, make four symmetrical holes, in a square shape, one on each corner, around 5mm (¼ in.) from the edge of the circle. Make one more hole in the centre of the circle (there will be a mark from the compass).

Making the middle arm

2 Cut a 12cm (4¾ in.) length of cotton thread for the middle hanging arm. Make a knot at the bottom, cut a tiny square of foil and wrap it around. Thread on one of the beads and then a piece of straw and another bead.

3 Gather together a set of ten of the Carnation Flower layers. Thread the needle through the centre of the layers with the needle and thread, then through the card circle.

4 Thread on the remaining ten layers of tissue paper, and finish with a bead. Push them all down to sit on the card circle. Make a knot on top and trim the thread. Cover the knot with a tiny square of foil and form into a ball.

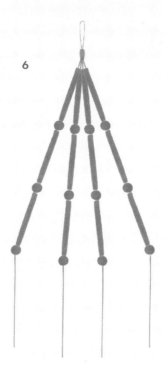

6

Making the upper arms and lower arms

5 Cut two 50cm (19½ in.) lengths of thread. Holding them together, fold the threads in half, and make a knot 5cm (2 in.) from the folded end to form a loop. You need this loop to be able to hang the pająk. You should then have four loose ends of thread for your arms.

6 Thread the needle onto the first arm, then thread on three pieces of straw, with a bead between each piece, then finish with a bead. Thread the other three arms in the same way.

7 When you have threaded the fourth arm, do not remove the needle, instead pull it through one of the holes in the card circle, then thread it with a bead and another piece of straw. This creates a lower arm. Finish with another bead. Make a knot at the bottom. Trim the thread, cut out a tiny square of foil and wrap it around the knot. Continue in the same way with the remaining three arms.

7

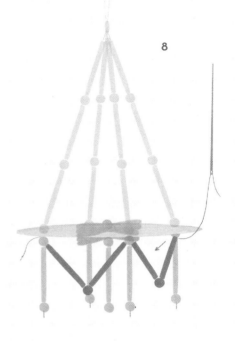

8

Making the lower hanging arms

8 Cut a 50cm (19½ in.) piece of thread for the lower dangling arms. Attach the end of the thread between the paper circle and one of the beads at the top of one of the lower arms. Thread the needle onto the loose end, then thread on a piece of straw, a bead and then another straw. Wrap the thread above the bead of the next lower arm, again underneath the paper circle. Repeat to make a second arm.

9 Once you have threaded all four arms, attach the last one under the card circle where you started and make a knot.

Tip You can really experiment with this design. Instead of straw you can just use beads, or rather than card circles, you can use a different shape, like a star, or whatever you like! You can also add more arms and more decorations.

BABY'S NURSERY MOBILE

This delicate, colourful mobile is perfect for a child's room. You can adorn it with your favourite toys, cartoon characters, beads or craft materials. The birds on my pająk were inspired by traditional shapes of birds from folk pottery.

Length 50cm (19¾ in.) · **Width** 30cm (12 in.)

What you will need

Coloured card
Bird template (p190)
Ruler
Scissors
Coloured paper drinking
  straws
2 x 30cm (12 in.) wooden
  5mm (¼ in.) dowel rods
Pencil
Cotton crochet thread
Ric rac trim
Glue
Needle
17 felt balls
Crepe paper in four
  different colours

Before you start

Cut out birds from bird template (p190):
20 from coloured card

Cut pieces of paper straw:
10 pieces of different lengths 3–8cm (1¼ –3¼ in.)

Note I used seven different colours of card for my birds. Each bird is made of two pieces so you can choose a different colour for each side, to make a multi-coloured bird.

Structure of the PAJĄK

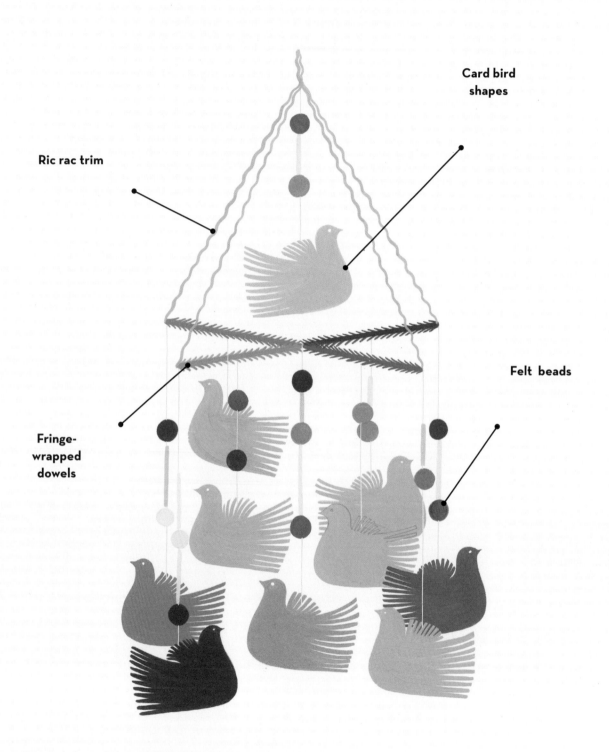

Card bird
shapes

Ric rac trim

Felt beads

Fringe-
wrapped
dowels

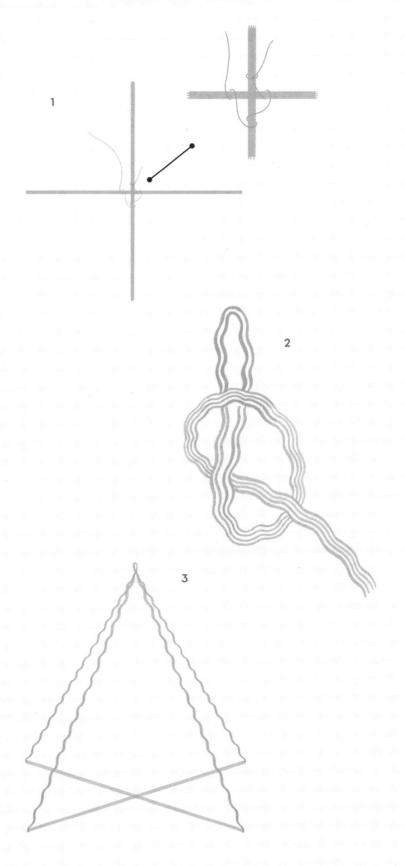

Making the cross arms

1 Prepare the two dowel rods by making a pencil mark in the middle of each one. Cut a 30cm (12 in.) length of thread. Hold both dowels side by side, wrap the thread around the middle where the marks are, and make a strong double knot. Turn the dowels, opening them up so that they make a cross shape, and wrap the thread around all four pieces, over the dowel, then under the dowel, so that they stay in place.

Making the upper arms

2 Cut two 70cm (27½ in.) lengths of ric rac trim, hold the pieces together, fold in half and create a loop on top by making a knot, to form four arms.

3 Check that the length of each arm is equal, then wrap each loose end of the trim around the four ends of dowel and glue them into place.

Making the birds

4 Cut ten 35cm (13¾ in.) lengths of thread. Place the 20 coloured card birds out on the surface in front of you. Apply glue to one of the birds, leaving the feather area clear (as marked on the template). Place a piece of thread down onto the glued area, with about 4cm (1½ in.) of thread inside the bird, then stick another bird on top.

5 Hold the two layers tightly together. Make cuts to the dotted line to create feathers on the top and down the back of the bird. Be careful not to cut off the thread that is sandwiched between the layers. Pull the two layers of feathers apart slightly so that they look nice and fluffy. Using a needle, make a hole to create an eye. Make nine more birds in the same way.

6 Once you have all the birds ready, thread each of their threads with felt balls and pieces of coloured paper straw. I hung each bird at a different height, so there are no rules about how to decorate each thread. Make some of them longer, with more straws and felt balls and some shorter, with only one ball. Hang the structure, so it is easier to add the birds.

5

7

8

7 Hang one bird between the upper arms, from the upper knot. This will need to be one with a shorter thread. Thread a needle, pull it through the top knot, wrap it twice and make a knot to secure it. Attach a bird to the middle of the wooden cross; this one could be on a longer thread. Add a bird to the end of each cross arm, at different heights but with quite long arms.

8 Attach four more birds, one to the middle of each cross arm, this time with shorter threads. Tie them on with a loose knot until you're sure about the placement. Cut off any excess thread.

9

151

CONTEMPORARY PAJAKI

Covering the cross arms
9 Cut four 30cm (12 in.) strips of crepe paper in different colours, each 3cm (1¼ in.) wide. Make 2cm (¾ in.) cuts close together along one edge of each strip. Glue the end of one of the strips to the outer end of one of the cross arms, cover the end and then wrap the arm up to the middle part of the cross, and glue in place.

10 Wrap each arm the same way using a different coloured strip. This will cover all the knots as well as making it look like a colourful carousel when your baby looks up at the mobile.

KIDS' PARTY PASTA PAJĄK

Who didn't like making pasta necklaces at school? Making a pasta pająk is a perfect way to spend time with the children in your life while having fun and learning some new skills.

Length 115cm (45¼ in.) • **Width** 45cm (17¾ in.)

What you will need

Crepe paper in different
  colours
Ruler
Scissors
Coloured card
5cm (2 in.) circle punch
  (optional)
Compass
Pencil
Foil
Wool yarn
Pompom template (p190)
40cm (15¾ in.) diameter
  metal hoop
Glue
Cotton crochet thread
5mm (¼ in.) ribbon

Dried pasta shapes:
  • small tubes, approx.
    1cm (½ in.), such as
    Canneroni
  • larger tubes, approx.
    4cm (1½ in.), such as
    Tortiglioni
  • Farfalle bows
Needle/plastic needles
  for kids
4 coloured pipe cleaners

Before you start

Make Paper Fans (p33):
  9 x 5cm (2 in.)
  8 x 6cm (2½ in.)
  17 x 7cm (2¾ in.)
  9 x 8cm (3¼ in.)

Cut card circles:
  8 x 5cm (2 in.)

Make 237 foil balls:
  scrunch up 3cm (1¼ in.)
  foil squares

**Make Wool Pompoms
(p64):** 7 x 8cm (3 in.)

Make Wool Tassels (p65):
  8 x 12cm (4¾ in.)

Structure of the PAJĄK

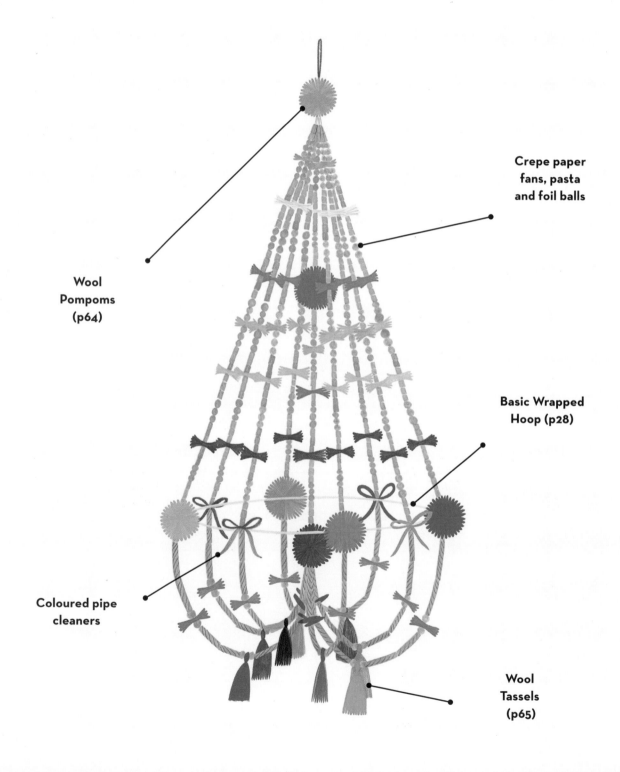

Crepe paper
fans, pasta
and foil balls

Wool
Pompoms
(p64)

Basic Wrapped
Hoop (p28)

Coloured pipe
cleaners

Wool
Tassels
(p65)

1 Wrap the hoop with cream crepe paper (p28).

Making the upper arms
2 Cut eight 90cm (35½ in.) lengths of thread. Make eight marks on the hoop with a pencil, first at the quarter points and then halfway between the quarter marks. Attach each of the threads to the hoop, wrapping them around the marked points and making a double knot.

3 This is a kids' party pająk so each thread can be arranged by the kids in whatever way they like. The order I followed is: six small pasta tubes, three foil balls, three small pasta tubes, navy blue 8cm (3¼ in.) paper fan, three small pasta tubes, three foil balls, three small pasta tubes, light blue 7cm (2¾ in.) paper fan, three small pasta tubes, three foil balls, bow pasta piece, three foil balls, three small pasta tubes, pink 6cm (2½ in.) paper fan, three small pasta tubes, three foil balls, three small pasta tubes, cream 5cm (2 in.) paper fan, three small pasta tubes, three foil balls, bow pasta piece, three foil balls, three small pasta tubes.

Tip The dried pasta bows break easily, so the kids might need help from an adult. Thread each bow through the middle, in an upwards direction.

4 Once all eight arms are threaded, gather them up at the top and make a strong double knot. Hang the pająk so that you can work on the lower parts more easily.

Making the lower arms

5 Cut eight 70cm (27½ in.) lengths of thread. Attach each one to the hoop, one under each of the upper arms. Each of my arms is threaded with: two long pasta tubes, foil ball, teal 7cm (2¾ in.) paper fan, foil ball, two large pasta tubes, foil ball, woollen tassel, foil ball, two large pasta tubes, foil ball, card circle, foil ball, two large pasta tubes. After threading the first of the lower arms, tie the loose end temporarily to the hoop. When you have threaded the second one, tie them up together. Continue with the rest of the arms.

6 Once all eight arms are threaded, gather them up at the bottom and make a strong double knot.

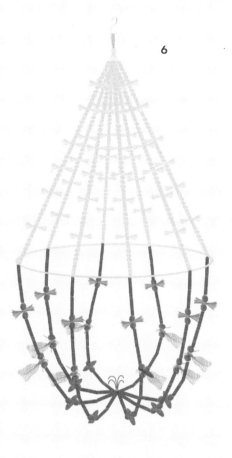

6

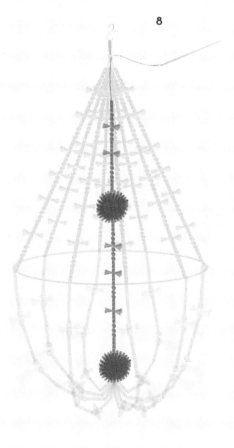

Making the middle arm

7 Cut a 1.8m (2 yd) length of thread. Fold it in half, thread a needle through and make a double knot at the bottom. Pull it through the knot of the lower hanging arms from underneath. Pull the needle through the middle of a woollen pompom, pushing it all the way down to the knot.

8 Then thread the central arm. I used: six small pasta tubes, three foil balls, three small pasta tubes, green 8cm (3 in.) paper fan, three small pasta tubes, three foil balls, three small pasta tubes, pink 7cm (2¾ in.) paper fan, three small pasta tubes, three foil balls, bow pasta piece, three foil balls, three small pasta tubes, wool pompom, three small pasta tubes, three foil balls, three small pasta tubes, cream 5cm (2 in.) paper fan, three small pasta tubes, three foil balls, bow pasta piece, three foil balls, finishing with three small pasta tubes.

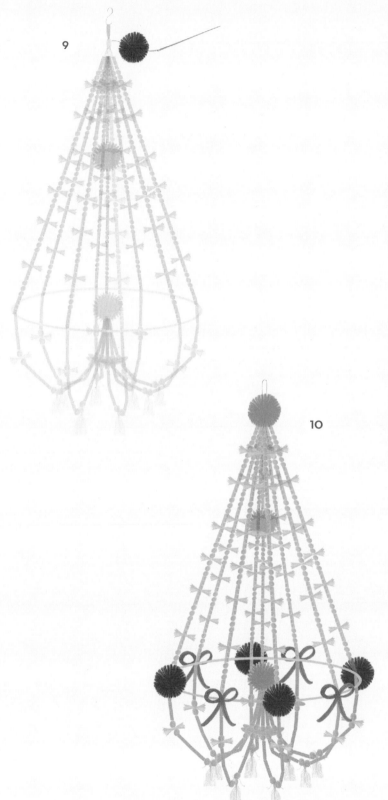

9 Pull the needle through the top knot twice, so it's secure. Pull the needle through another wool pompom and push it down to the knot. Cut a 30cm (12 in.) length of ribbon, and fold it in half to create a loop. Cut off the needle and attach the ribbon loop with one of the threads. Then make a strong double knot on top. Cut off any excess thread.

10 Attach the final four wool pompoms to the hoop at quarter points and between them add the coloured pipe cleaners - wrap them around the hoop and form into a bow shape.

WEDDING CHANDELIER

This is a simple, minimalist structure built with ribbons. Choose any flowers you love in your favourite colours. For this one, I chose hydrangeas and baby's breath (gypsophila) for their beautiful colours and textures. I have also made pająki with peonies and thistles and I loved how they dried out. It's like a living sculpture. This will look stunning as a centrepiece for your wedding. Congratulations!

Length 90cm (35½ in.) · **Width** 70cm (27½ in.) with flowers!

What you will need

50cm (19½ in.) metal hoop
25mm (1 in.) grosgrain
   ribbon, in two different
   colours (I used light and
   dark green), around 15m
   (16½ yd) in total
Scissors
Measuring tape
Pencil
Fresh flowers
Strong fabric glue
Florist wire

Structure of the PAJĄK

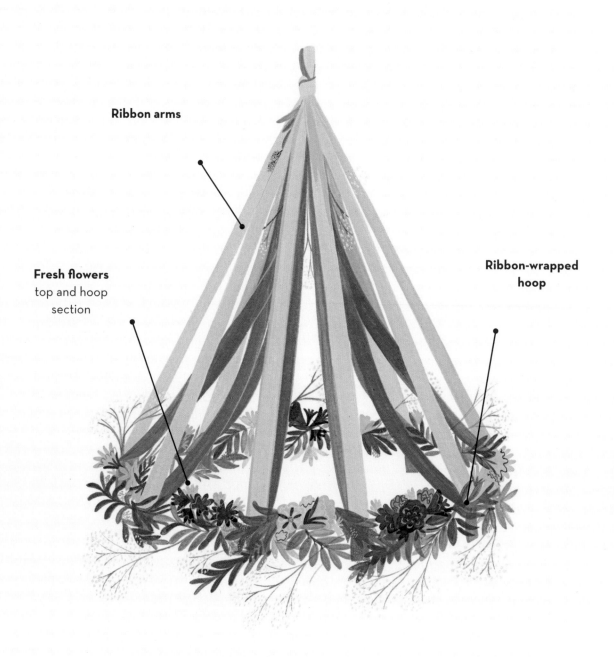

Ribbon arms

Fresh flowers
top and hoop
section

**Ribbon-wrapped
hoop**

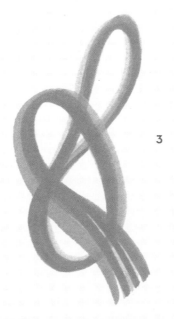

3

1 Wrap the hoop, using ribbon instead of crepe paper (p28).

Making the outer ribbon arms

2 Make eight pencil marks on the hoop, first at the quarter points, and then divide each quarter in half, so there are eight marks, spaced equally.

Making the inner ribbon arms

3 Cut four 1.5m (1¾ yd) lengths of lighter green ribbon and four 2m (2¼ yd) lengths of darker green ribbon. Fold both sets in half, with the longer ribbons inside the shorter ones, and then make a knot just under the fold to create a loop on the top. In my design, the darker green ribbons are inside the structure so when folding the ribbon I put them inside. Check that the two sets of ribbons are even; you can trim some of them if necessary.

4 Attach the eight outer ribbons to the hoop (these are the shorter, lighter green ones). Start by attaching four of the ribbons at the quarter marks around the hoop, then continue with the other four. Wrap the end of each ribbon around the hoop and glue it. Hold it tight to fix it in place.

5 Next, attach the inside eight arms (the longer, darker green ones). They should hang nicely inside the structure. Glue them to the inside of the lighter green arms. You will need to leave 15cm (6 in.) of the dark green ribbon dangling below the hoop, as shown. Apply glue to the hoop, on top of the wrapped light green ribbon, and stick down the inside ribbon 15cm (6 in.) from the end. Press it tight so it stays in place.

Attaching the flowers

6 Decorate your ribbon pająk with any flowers you like. Use florist wire to attach different flowers all the way around the hoop.

7 Finally, attach a few flowers to the top knot, so they are hanging down inside the structure.

+ Józef +

High on the top of a hill in the Tatra Mountains in southern Poland is a traditional wooden house where Józef Fudala has lived since he was born.

I visited him in early winter and when I entered his house, the first thing I noticed were paper Christmas tree chains hanging everywhere. He was busy preparing decorations for Christmas.

His mother taught him paper craft. He worked very hard on his farm all his life and since his retirement he's spent his time making paper flowers and other traditional decorations.

All around me I could see piles of beautifully embroidered cushions, hand-painted tapestries hanging on the walls and paintings of saints decorated with Józef's paper flowers. Looking at all these treasures, I felt like I was in an ethnographic museum.

Walking into each room was like entering the world of Narnia. The last one was his 'white room', or *biała izba*; in the past, this was the most grand and important room in the traditional, rural house and where you entertained guests. In Józef's house, this room was decorated entirely with his paper creations. I imagine the festive period lasts a whole year here as the three faux Christmas trees are permanent fixtures. These are decorated with beautiful paper angels made by his grandmother as well as other traditional Christmas decorations, such as long rye-straw chains with colourful paper fans, and beautiful paper flowers in the shape of pine cones.

Józef's hedgehog pompoms are one of a kind. Traditionally, these pompoms were added to decorate the pająk structure and used as single Christmas baubles. I've seen them made in all different colours but I fell in love with Józef's ones as soon as I saw them. He uses white paper to make them and then adds aluminium foil for each spike.

Everywhere you look there are Józef's hedgehog pompoms, attached to the Christmas trees and suspended from the ceiling. They look incredible, as if this magical space is filled with glinting snowflakes.

SNOWY CHRISTMAS PAJĄK

This is my homage to the lovely Józef. It is smaller in scale than some of the other projects, but is still a very magical pająk featuring my favourite white Hedgehog Pompoms with their silver spikes.

Length 42cm (16½ in.) • **Width** 22cm (8½ in.)

What you will need

Rye or paper straw
Ruler
Scissors
Foil
White tissue paper
Compass
Pencil
Pencil sharpener
Needle
Glue
Cotton crochet thread
20cm (8 in.) diameter
  metal hoop
White metallic crepe
  paper

Before you start

Cut pieces of straw:
  32 x 3cm (1¼ in.)
  18 x 5cm (2 in.)

Make 42 foil balls:
  scrunch up 3cm (1¼ in.)
  foil squares

Prepare the layers for Józef's Hedgehog Pompom (p45):
  1 x 7cm (2¾ in.) with 12 layers

Make Józef's Hedgehog Pompoms (p45):
  4 x 7cm (2¾ in.) with 8 layers

Structure of the PAJĄK

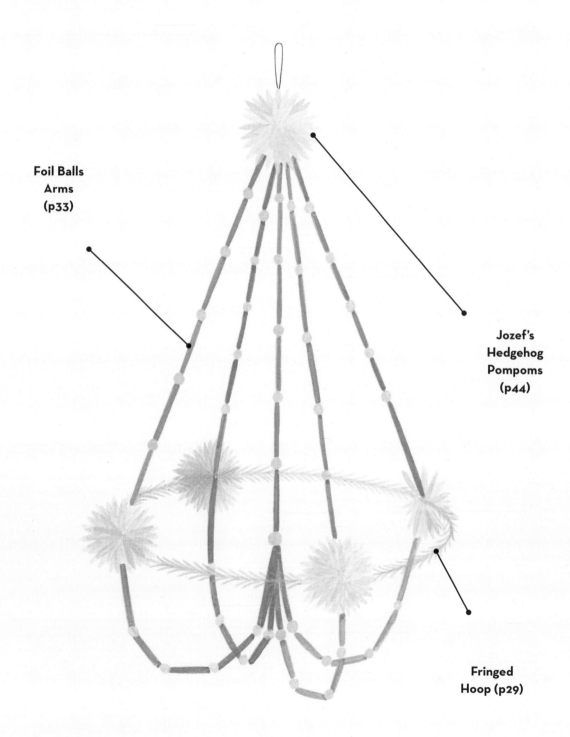

**Foil Balls
Arms
(p33)**

**Jozef's
Hedgehog
Pompoms
(p44)**

**Fringed
Hoop (p29)**

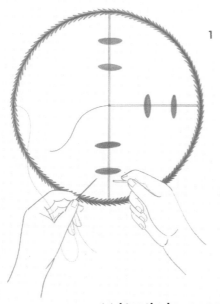

1

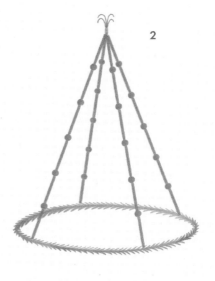

2

1 Wrap the hoop in a fringe style with white metallic crepe paper (p29).

Making the upper arms
2 Cut four 45cm (17¾ in.) lengths of thread. Attach them to the hoop at the quarter points. Tie each one around the hoop with a double knot. Using a needle, thread one of the arms with a long piece of straw, followed by four short straws and then another long one, with five foil balls in between. Repeat the same process for the remaining three arms. Gather the loose ends together and make a strong knot. Hang your pająk so you can work on the lower parts.

Making the lower arms
3 Cut four more 45cm (17¾ in.) lengths of thread. Attach them to the hoop at the points where the upper arms are attached. Thread each lower arm with a long straw, followed by three short ones, finishing with a long one, threading four foil balls in between. After threading the first of the lower arms, tie the loose end temporarily to the hoop. When you have threaded the second one, tie them up together. Once you have two sets of two arms ready, gather them all together and make a final knot.

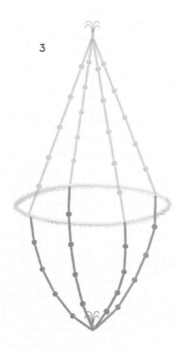

3

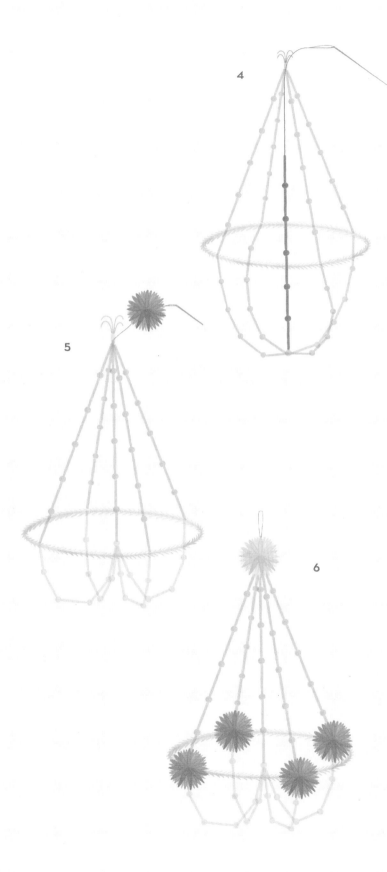

Making the central arm

4 Cut a 90cm (35½ in.) length of thread, thread a needle and make a knot at the bottom. Pull the needle through the knot that joins the lower arms, from underneath. Thread on a foil ball, then a long piece of straw, four short ones and then finish with a long one, attaching five foil balls in between. Pull the needle through the top knot where the upper arms are joined.

5 Thread the 12 layers of the top Józef's Hedgehog Pompom onto the needle and push down onto the central arm thread. Cut a small pad of tissue paper, pull it through and push it down inside the pompom. Cut a 15cm (6 in.) length of cotton thread. Fold it in half and make a double knot at the bottom to create a loop. Attach it inside the pompom with the one of the threads and then make a double knot on top. Cut off any excess thread.

6 Attach the final four Hedgehog Pompoms to the sides – tie them tightly to the hoop. One thread goes above the hoop, the other one under, and then tie them with a double knot.

MACRAMÉ PAJĄK FOR PLANTS

This is a lovely contemporary version of a pająk for pompom, plant and macramé lovers!

Length 75cm (29½ in.) · **Width** 35cm (13¾ in.)

What you will need

Rye or paper straw

Ruler

Scissors

Coloured card in teal, brown and turquoise

3cm (1¼ in.) circle punch (optional)

Compass

Pencil

Pencil sharpener

Tissue paper in teal and light brown

Needle

Glue

Cotton crochet thread

Foil

30cm (12 in.) diameter brass hoop

Jute twine string

Four ceramic plant pots (8cm/3¼ in. diameter)

Four of your favourite plants to fit the pots

Before you start

Cut pieces of straw:
58 x 3cm (1¼ in.)
26 x 8cm (3¼ in.)

Cut card circles:
71 x 3cm (1¼ in.)

Prepare the layers for Hedgehog Pompoms (p42):
2 x 10cm (4 in.), one in teal and one in mixed colours

Make Hedgehog Pompoms (pp42–43):
4 x 10cm (4 in.) in light brown

Structure of the PAJĄK

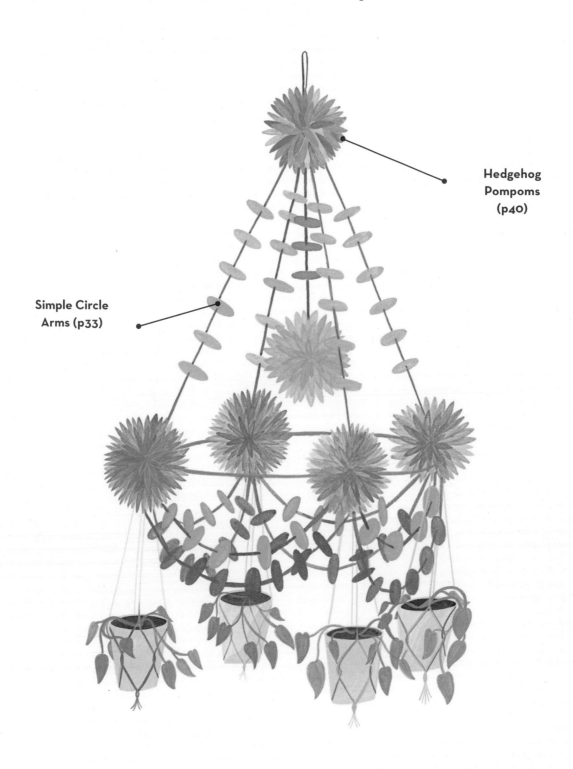

Hedgehog
Pompoms
(p40)

Simple Circle
Arms (p33)

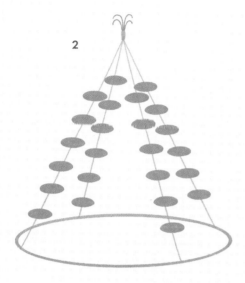

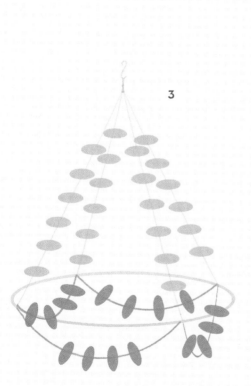

Making the upper arms

1 Prepare the hoop. Cut four 50cm (19½ in.) lengths of cotton thread. Attach them to the hoop, at the quarter points. Wrap the threads around the hoop and make a double knot. The hoop is not wrapped with paper, so use glue to hold them in place.

2 Thread the needle onto the loose end of one of the arms and thread on a long piece of straw, followed by five shorter ones, finishing with another long one, and adding six card circles in between. Continue to thread the rest of arms in the same way. Once all the arms are finished, gather them together and make a knot at the top. Check if the hoop hangs straight. Adjust if not, then make a second strong knot. Hang the pająk so you can work on the lower parts.

Making two sets of lower dangling arms

3 Cut four 50cm (19½ in.) pieces of thread for the first set of four dangling arms. Wrap the first thread around the hoop, at the point where one of the upper arms is attached to the hoop, make a knot and thread with a long straw, three short ones and then another long straw, with four card circles in between. Attach the end of the thread to the hoop, under the next upper arm. Wrap it around and make a double knot. Continue with the remaining three threads.

Tip If you don't want to attach each arm separately, you can cut a longer piece of thread, and then thread all arms in one go, extending the thread if you need to by knotting on an extra piece of thread.

4 Cut four 70cm (27½ in.) pieces of cotton thread for another set of lower dangling arms. Attach them to the hoop, under the shorter ones, in the same way. Thread a long piece of straw first, then six short ones, finishing with another long one, with seven card discs in between.

Making the macramé pot holders

5 Cut four 90cm (35½ in.) lengths of jute string for each pot holder. Hold a set together, thread them through the hoop (where the upper and lower arms are attached). Adjust the ends so the hoop is sitting halfway along the strings, and tie them onto the hoop. You should have eight strings to work with. Tie on three more sets.

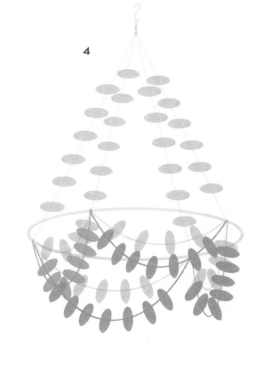

4

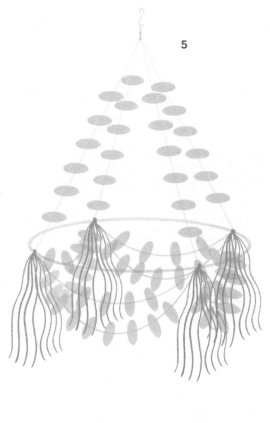

5

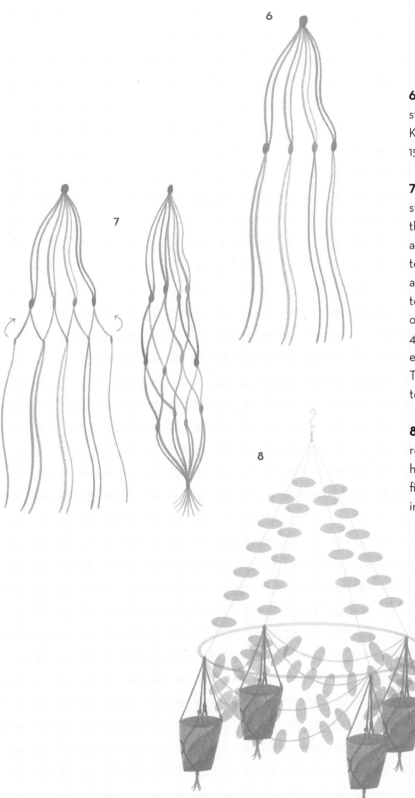

6 Separate the eight strings into four pairs. Knot the pairs about 15cm (6 in.) down.

7 Now, knot two more strings together, each of them from another pair, as shown. Don't forget to knot the furthest left and right strings together too. Repeat the process once more, leaving about 4cm (1½ in.) between each section of knots. Then knot all the strings together and trim them.

8 Repeat to make the remaining three pot holders. When you are finished, insert a pot into each holder.

Adding the pompoms

9 Gather together the 24 layers for the two Hedgehog Pompoms. Cut an 80cm (31½ in.) length of thread, thread the needle, fold it in half and make a double knot. Cut a tiny square of foil, wrap it around the knot and squeeze it into a ball. Thread on 12 of the teal layers, changing the directions of the spikes. Push the layers down to the knot. Cut a tiny square (7mm/¼ in.) of foil, wrap it around the thread and push it down the pompom so it stays in a round shape.

10 Thread on a long straw, followed by two short ones and finish with a long one, with three card discs in between. Pull the needle through the top knot, wrap it twice to secure it. Thread the other 12 layers to complete the top Hedgehog Pompom. I made a rainbow one, so I used six teal and six pale brown layers. Cut out a small square pad of tissue, thread it onto the needle and push it down the pompom. Cut off the needle, and make a strong double knot.

11 Cut a 25cm (10cm) length of jute string, fold it in half and make a loop by making a knot at the bottom. Attach it inside the pompom. Holding the two threads, make a strong double knot to secure the structure. Cut off any excess string.

12 Attach the remaining Hedgehog Pompoms to the hoop. Wrap one thread over the hoop, another one under, and then make a strong double knot. Cut off any excess thread.

Adding the plants

13 Put your plants into the holder – making sure that the hoop stays well balanced. I decided on Devil's Ivy but any kind of succulent will look great!

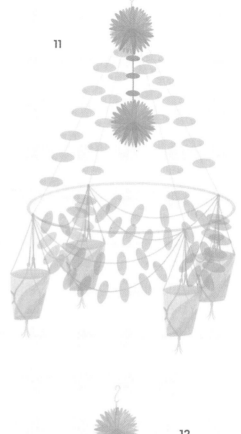

12

BRASS STAR SCULPTURE

This is a contemporary version of a traditional pająk design. Instead of pieces of rye straw, I used brass tubes. Without the addition of the usual paper flowers or pompoms, it looks like a minimal sculpture.

Length 49cm (19 in.) · **Width** 48cm (19 in.)

What you will need

5mm (¼ in.) brass tubes
Tube cutter (optional)
Florist wire
Pliers

Before you start

If you can't buy pre-cut brass tubes in the desired length you can cut them yourself using a tube cutter.

Cut lengths of brass tube:
36 x 6cm (2¼ in.)
72 x 12cm (4¾ in.)

Structure of the PAJĄK

Outer pyramids

Inner
structure

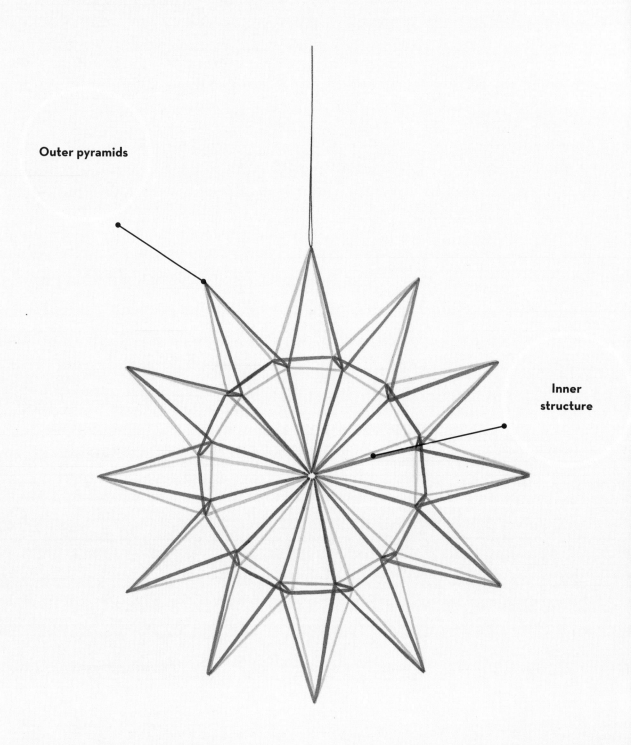

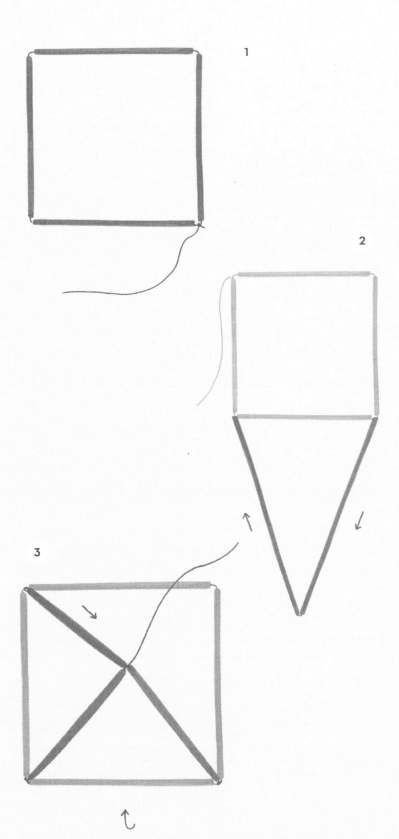

Note The structure is built from 12 threaded pyramids inside, with 12 extra pyramids added around the outside. The whole structure is threaded using the wire. Cut 50cm (19½ in.) lengths of wire. When you run out of wire, cut another piece and wrap them tightly together.

Making the inner structure

1 Cut the first 50cm (19½ in.) length of wire. Thread four short brass tubes onto the wire to form a square. Wrap the two wires at the corner around one another so the square base is secure.

2 Now you need to build a pyramid on top. Take the long piece of wire at the corner, and thread on two long tubes. Fold this into a triangle shape, and wrap the wire under the corner to attach it to the square. Then pull the wire through the tube to the other corner of the square, as shown.

3 Thread another long tube onto the wire. Wrap the wire around the top of the first triangle to build the pyramid.

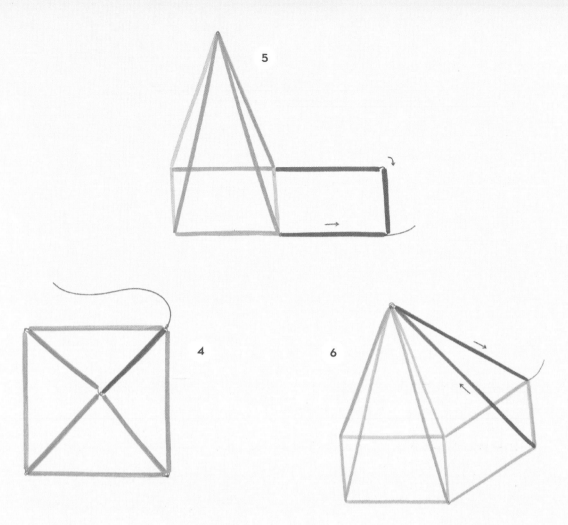

4 Then add another long tube in the same way to finish the structure. Wrap the wire under the lower corner to secure it. You now have one pyramid module ready.

5 You need to add 11 more modules to build the star structure. Add three short tubes to the lower base to form a second square. Wrap the wire round at the bottom of the first pyramid and thread back through the tube as shown.

6 To build the pyramid you will only need to add two more long tubes, attaching them to the top of the first pyramid. Add the first tube, pull it to the side and wrap the wire under the top of the first pyramid. Add the second tube and wrap the wire round at the bottom, as shown.

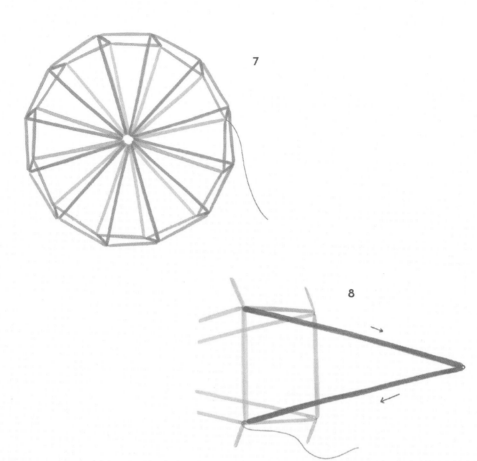

7

8

7 Continue to make ten more pyramids until you have closed the middle structure. The last two pieces you need to add will be two short tubes at the bottom to connect the first and the last pyramid. It might look a bit messy as you are working, but if you make sure you pull the wire quite tight in the middle of the structure, it will look great in the end.

Tip Remember, if you need to thread the wire to the other side of a shape, pull it through the tube. Don't leave any ends visible. It looks better when the structure is neat.

Adding the outer pyramids
8 Once you have the middle structure ready you need to attach the 12 outer 'spiky' pyramids. There should be a piece of wire coming out from the square base, where you finished the middle layer. Extend the length of the wire if necessary and thread on two more long tubes.

9 Pull the wire through the bottom short tube.

10 Add a long tube and wrap it under the triangle top to create a pyramid. Add another long tube to finish the pyramid.

11 Continue with the remaining 11 pyramids. Once you have built all of the pyramids your star is ready to hang!

Tip You can change the lengths of the tubes to change the appearance of your star. If you want longer 'spiky' pyramids, you can use longer tubes.

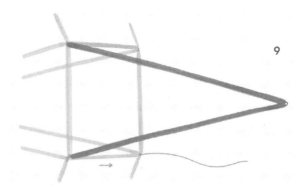

9

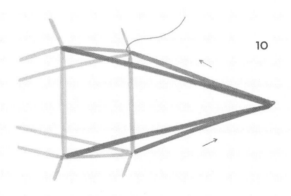

10

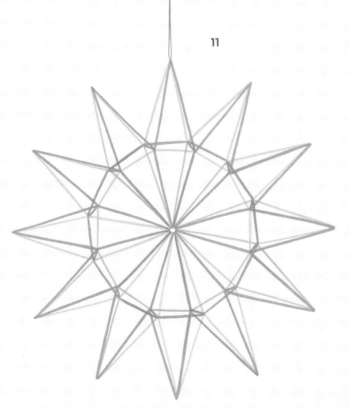

11

Templates

Use tracing paper, photocopy the templates or scan them
and print at 100%. Alternatively, download the templates from:
www.pavilionbooks.com/book/making-mobiles

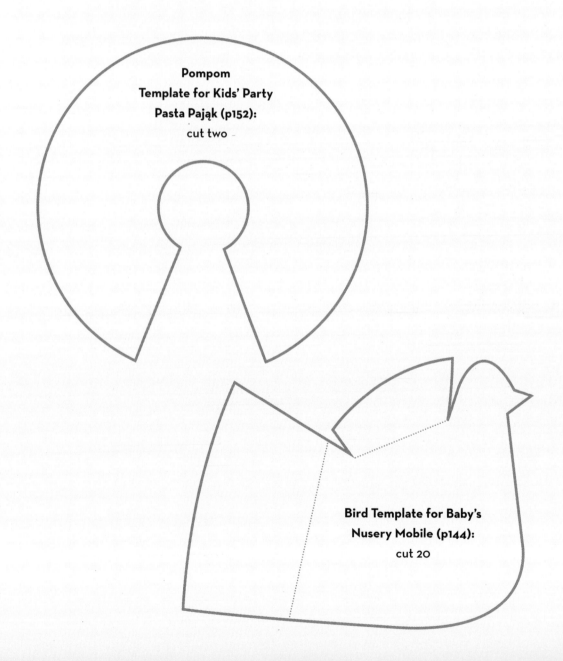

**Pompom
Template for Kids' Party
Pasta Pająk (p152):**
cut two

**Bird Template for Baby's
Nusery Mobile (p144):**
cut 20

Suppliers

Karolina Merska

www.karolinamerska.com

This is my own website! You can buy a pająk DIY kit direct from me with all the paper and straw you need to make your own at home.

Atlantis Art Materials

www.atlantisart.co.uk

My local art store. Great selection of papers.

Cass Art

www.cassart.co.uk

Online art store perfect for papers and tools. Lots of branches across the UK.

G. F. Smith

www.gfsmith.com

London-based company supplying card and papers in amazing colours.

Carte Fini

www.cartefini.com

Italian crepe paper in beautiful colours.

Fred Aldous

www.fredaldous.co.uk

Online shop perfect for all your crafty needs. You'll find metal hoops, paper punches and everything else to start making your pająki. They have two shops in the UK, in Leeds and Manchester.

Great Art

www.greatart.co.uk

Online art store perfect for papers and tools. With a stationery shop in the UK (London).

Further reading

It wasn't easy to research a history of pająki as there is not a lot of material written about them. I am lucky to own a book, *Podłaźniki* by Tadeusz Seweryn, from 1932, which is a great source of information filled with unique illustrations and photographs. Also, I would like to mention two very important publications by Tomasz Czerwiński, *Wyposażenie domu wiejskiego w Polsce* (*Interiors of the Countryside House in Poland*), and Aleksander Jackowski, *Polska sztuka ludowa* (*Polish Folk Art*). While writing the book I had the pleasure of meeting Professor Marian Pokropek, whose books on Polish folk art I read and recommend: *Ludowe tradycje Suwalszczyzny* (*Folk Traditions in Suwalszczyzna*), and especially his large publication *Folk Art in Poland* (available in English), which he wrote together with Ewa Fryś and Anna Iracka.

Thank You

To Gemma Doyle, Bella Cockrell and Katie Cowan from Pavilion Books, without whose support and trust this book would not have been possible. Also to Claire Clewley and Amy Christian for their enormous help with the layout and copy edit.

To Ola O. Smit, photographer and a dear friend, for the beautiful photos.

To Georgie Ellen McAusland for the wonderful drawings.

To the artists: Zofia Samul, Helena Półtorak and Józef Fudala for sharing their knowledge.

To Professor Marian Pokropek for a research meeting and discussion not just about pająki craft.

To Renata i Wojciech Brzozowscy from the Folk Museum of the Brzozowski's family in Sromów in Poland for an inspiring tour.

To Vero, Kasia, Esther and Elisa for their help in the studio.

To Piers Martin for his advice on my writing.

To my parents; Małgorzata for helping cut the straw and Mirosław for driving me to visit the artists. To sisters Alicja and Magdalena for their love and support.

To all you pająki lovers for your excitement about pająki, joining my workshops here in London or writing to me from around the world. Without you this book wouldn't have happened at all!